## WHAT *FATHERS* ARE SAYING ABOUT THIS BOOK

"Pursuing custody was like trying to navigate uncharted waters! The insight I received by reading this book allowed me to utilize precise information to stay the very stormy and unpredictable course with patience and integrity thus allowing me to reach calm waters with my son and my self respect in tact."
**RICHARD L. MADDON – Fullerton, California**

"The key to success in any custody battle is to read this book before divorce proceedings to avoid costly mistakes. I followed the strategies outlined and got custodial rights for my two sons."
**PETER J. BECK – Newport Beach, California**

"Finally, a practical approach to making sense for the complexity of family law court. *Custody for Fathers* made the difference between winning and losing my own custody case, proud father of Cory and Sarah."
**RICK SMITH - Irvine, California**

" The Brennan's book helped me to design a game plan for my own custody case by keeping an open mind as to options, choices, and alternatives. It's nice to have an attorney with integrity on your side."
**MARTIN STUKA – Newport Beach, California**

"If more non-custodial parents had this book in their hands before a court hearing, more children in our society would have equal and open access to both parents. This book is a must have."
**TED HILL - Riverside, California**

"I have just finished reading your book and my biggest regret is that I didn't have this book in my hands eleven months ago."
**DAVE LEWIS - Hudson, New Hampshire**

"I found the tools and techniques used in your book invaluable. Your style of writing is straightforward, and easy to understand. I highly recommend this book be read by anyone going into a court battle."
**PETER WILLIAM CABRAL - Joshua Tree, California**

"I followed your instructions in the mediation chapter, and by using the techniques learned, the mediator recommended everything I wanted."
**RICHARD WALDROP - Brookin, Maine**

# WHAT *AUTHORS* ARE SAYING ABOUT THIS BOOK

# WHAT *JOURNALISTS* ARE SAYING ABOUT THIS BOOK

"The definitive book for fathers and attorneys."
**DAVID BACH** - *Man Talk,* **Radio Show**
**Phoenix, Arizona**

"A custody battle plan that takes no prisoners."
**LYNN SMITH** - *Los Angeles Times,* **Newspaper**
**Los Angeles, California**

"Written brilliantly. The courts owe children time with their fathers. This book is a step in the right direction."
**KAREN ROWAN** - *Hispana News,* **Newspaper**
**Colorado Springs, Colorado**

"Fathers facing divorce would do well to read this book. Maybe the kids could emerge the winners."
**MIKE PETERSON** - *Press Republican,* **Newspaper**
**Plattsburgh, New York**

"This book helps fathers learn how to work within the legal system, teaching them how to deal with judges and courts, and how to present themselves as good role model for their kids."
**DON HUNTER** - *The Province,* **Newspaper**
**Vancouver, Canada**

"This self-published title is a practical, and important manual written to guide readers through a custody battleground. Although mothers here are considered 'the enemy,' the book does provide an unusual viewpoint covering tricks of manipulation and keys to succeeding as a non-custodial parent."
**DIANE DONOVAN** - *Midwest Book Review*
**Oregon, Wisconsin**

# WHAT *ORGANIZATIONS* ARE SAYING ABOUT THIS BOOK

"Buy this book" it will help non-custodial parents maintain a loving and meaningful relationship with their children."
**CHILDREN'S RIGHTS COUNSEL - David Levy, President**
**Washington, D.C.**

"A must read for any father or father's attorney who is planning to advocate for father-custody. The chapter on Basic Strategies and Tactics alone is worth many times the cost of this book."
**F.R.E.E. FOUNDATION - Anne Mitchell, Attorney, Founder**
**Santa Clara, California**

"I'm writing to tell you how impressed I am with your book. I use your book as a teaching tool for my organization 'My Child Says Daddy.' I deal with thousands of fathers a year."
**MY CHILD SAYS DADDY - Reginald Brass, President**
**Los Angeles, California**

"This book contains excellent information that can save dads time, emotional pain, and money in legal fees. The only book I have ever offered for sale in this office in the 10 years of the DRC's existance."
**DOMESTIC RIGHTS COALITION - George Gilliland**
**St. Paul, Minnesota**

"Only book I've seen that shows a father how to conduct himself within the art of the judicial arena through words, actions and body language. A father is methodically moved through the courthouse, mediation, and the judge to familiarize him with the elements of a custody battle."
**FATHERS FOR EQUAL RIGHTS - K.C. Ward**
**Denver, Colorado**

"In the 20 years I have been involved with men and divorce issues, I have never seen a better guide for men."
**NATIONAL COALITION OF FREE MEN - Tom Williamson, President.**
**Manhasset, New York**

# WHAT *ORGANIZATIONS* ARE SAYING ABOUT THIS BOOK

"Invaluable information about the custody process and legal system written in a very easy-to-read and easy-to reference format."
**FATHERS FOR EQUALITY EXCHANGE - (F.R.E.E.) - Bob Kass**
**Madison, Wisconsin**


"*Custody for Fathers* is an essential 'crash-course' guide to getting you through the legal system. An in-your-face book helping you to comprehend how a litigant is viewed by decision-making others - attorneys, judges, therapists and opposition. Right-on in guiding you in your conduct, case, and goals to get the most favorable reaction from those deciding the fate of you and your children."
**JOINT CUSTODY ASSOCIATION - James A. Cook, President**
**Los Angeles, California**


"This book belongs on the desk of any father who genuinely wants to win custody of his children. I consider this the best book on the subject since Charlie Metz's, Divorce and Custody for Men, which has been out of print for over 25 years."
**MEN'S DEFENSE ASSOCIATION - Richard Doyle, President**
**Forrest Lake, Minnesota**


"Crucial to a court custody battle is your book. Hopefully the day will arrive when *Custody for Fathers* will not longer be an important resource for fathers seeking fair play in the custody wars. Until that day arrives, your book is a wonderful resource and I would say to any father - don't go to court without it."
**COALITION OF PARENT SUPPORT - Robert Chandler, Past President**
**Modesto, California**

# WARNING - DISCLAIMER

This book is not intended to replace attorneys. The information in this book is designed to provide guidance for a father in custody litigation. We urge you to read all of the material in this book and learn as much as possible about the legal system, how it works, and consequences thereof.

Every effort has been made to make this book as complete and accurate as possible. This text should be used only as a guide to winning custody of your children. The publishers and authors shall have neither liability nor responsibility to any person or entity with respect to any loss or damage caused, or alleged to be caused directly or indirectly by the information in this book

# CUSTODY
# *for*
# FATHERS

---

*A practical guide*
*through*
*the combat zone of a brutal custody battle*

---

**Fourth Revised Edition**

**Carleen Brennan**
*and*
**Michael Brennan, Attorney at Law**
**250 East 17th Street**
**Costa Mesa, CA. 92627**
**(949) 646-9842**
**(949) 646-3453 - Fax**

# CUSTODY FOR FATHERS
A practical guide through the combat zone
of a brutal custody battle

By Carleen Brennan & Michael Brennan

Published by:
BRENNAN PUBLISHING
250 East 17th Street
Costa Mesa, CA. 92627 U.S.A.

Copyright 1994
First Printing -1994
Second Printing 1996 revised
Third Printing    1998 revised
Fourth Printing 1999 revised
Printed in the United States of America

Library of Congress Cataloging-in-Publication Data
Brennan, Carleen and Michael
        Custody for Fathers, a practical guide through the combat zone of a brutal custody battle / by Carleen and Michael Brennan 4th rev.ed.
        p.cm.

ISBN 0-9644157-4-0

1. Divorce   2.  Law    3.  Self-Help

# DEDICATED
## to


## the thousands of children
## we have touched

## And

## the millions of children
## we now reach out to

# ACKNOWLEDGMENTS

We acknowledge those fathers who have been through the wringer of a brutal custody battle. Their stories and experiences are the foundation on which this book has been written. These pioneering fathers have led the way in a societal trend that will one day be accepted as the standard - fathers can raise children, successfully.

We thank Steve Ball for giving up many evenings and weekends to help us with this project. Grateful appreciation is extended to Suzanne Ashe-Dudley for her literary guidance. Lucky were we to utilized the creative talents of Lin Alvarez, our graphic artist, who through all our changes, kept smiling. We also wish to thank Ken Halverson for his willingness to give up personal time to make this project a reality. And, in the stretch, when the number of pages made the manuscript unwieldy, Ryan Shook kept things manageable. To Megan for her ever-efficient performance. To the staff of Sir Rogers Sandwich Shop, for sustenance these past eleven months. To our wonderful children, Alix, Jason, Amy, and Ryan for their encouragement, patience, and love.

We have received overwhelming accolades from divorce professionals, news media, and fathers. Daily telephone calls from across the country, inform us that this book made the difference in a positive outcome in individual cases. We thank the thousands who have contributed toward the word-of-mouth promotion that has resulted in the need for a third printing.

## ABOUT THE AUTHORS

The authors are married and operate a law office that represents fathers in custody cases. Popular speakers on Television, radio, seminars and to divorce professionals. Twenty-four years in family law.

# TABLE OF CONTENTS

# INTRODUCTION

This book is about Children's Rights. The right of children to live with the parent who will devote time, expend the energy, and make the sacrifices necessary to mold the life of a child. Children deserve the right to be raised in the home of the better parent, no matter the gender. If a father is the better parent, then the children should live with him. The proper parent is the one who will teach children sound moral values, and help them to develop good character traits. Children and our nation will be much better served when the custodial parent is selected according to parenting skill level, not gender.

We are now on the cutting edge of a shift in society, from father/breadwinner and mother/homemaker, to both the parents working outside the home sharing equally in child raising. This societal change has progressed to a level where fathers are now taking a pro-active role in raising children: Meal preparation, bathing, helping with homework, planning social activities, and the thousands of chores necessary for healthy child development. Today's fathers are now participating fully in every aspect of the children's lives, tasks that for generations have been performed by mothers.

Think back to the beginning of mankind, and note how the family unit has evolved over the centuries. Mankind has adapted according to the culture and needs of the times. Primitive man lived in clans, indiscriminate sex meant the father could have been any member, and the children were raised by the whole clan. Mankind progressed out of the cave, into the fields, and children were needed to perform the arduous chores of working the fields. Farming without the use of machinery required extra laborers that encouraged multiple wives which resulted in large families. As society evolved from a farming based economy to a commerce driven era, the family became a much smaller unit, and polygamy no longer benefited economic existence.

We are now in the initial phase of a major transitional period in the evolvement of the family unit. Mothers working outside the homes have changed a century's old tradition of child development. Children are growing up in daycare centers. This shift in society means the custodial parent should be selected according to who will provide the better environment, as opposed to the historical preference for children to be raised by mothers. Laws need be enacted so that fathers are on an equal footing .

A study of chimpanzees, mans closest animal relation, concluded that parenting skills are not genetically imprinted in chimpanzee mothers, but are learned traits. This study questions the traditional thinking of children needing to be raised by their mothers. The Tender Years Doctrine is deeply ingrained in our culture, and in the minds of family law judges. Some judges favor the mother until a father proves mother has three eyes, breathes fire, and drinks swamp water. In spite of this mom bias, there have been many fathers who have convinced a judge that they were the better custodial parent for their children. **You can too.**

Gone are the days of Ozzie and Harriet, til death do us part, and moms stayed home baking apple pies. Easy divorce has changed the American way of life, and this nation is now a fatherless society. There are over one million divorces each year involving children, and mothers are granted custody in 90% of those cases. Statistics show that at least one-third of all children are living apart from their fathers, and in some cities the figure is over 50%. This national nightmare has disconnected children from fathers by a legal system that gives children no say in the matter.

Custody laws have not kept up with the needs of children when parents separate. Changes will come in the laws, but not in time to help your case. You cannot change the laws, so you must learn to use strategies and tactics that have worked for other fathers who have won custody. Working to change custody laws is a worthwhile effort, but should be reserved until after your court case is concluded, as your time will be better used on solving your current problems.

One out of four children is born of unwed parents. When couples are not married, the case is called a *Paternity Case* instead of *Dissolution Of Marriage*. Custody disputes in paternity cases are treated exactly the same as divorce cases by the family law court system. Therefore, whether you are married to the mother of your children, or not, everything in this book can be effectively used to get custody of your children.

When custody is disputed, court proceedings seldom go smoothly. Tensions are high, parents are on emotional overload, and the possibility of violence is real. A well-respected judge once said, *"A murder case doesn't have a fraction of the explosiveness of a bitter divorce case."*

The rights of children should exceed the rights of either parent. Government needs to get more concerned about the rights of children and less concerned about the civil rights of parents. Government must work toward keeping all fathers involved in the child raising after parents no longer live together. Today, if one partner wants out of a marriage, it is automatically granted. The family breakup is the beginning of a process that causes misery, pain, and suffering for children. Growing up without a father is an experience no child should have to endure.

Studies show that children living in homes without a father are:
- More disruptive in school.
- More violent.
- More criminal activities.
- More drug/alcohol usage.

This fatherlessness syndrome sets off a cycle of childhood misery which repeats itself in successive generations. Children in desperate situations do desperate things, and the result is little chance for a decent life. All children deserve to grow up with the guidance of a father.

Further studies indicate that children who have lost their father through death adjust much better than children who have lost contact with their biological father, because there is guilt and shame associated with an absent father. Absent fathers are an easy target for politicians who think that budgets can be balanced by way of child support payments. However, absent fathers do not have the money or resources to litigate in a system that is highly biased in favor of mothers.

Children Deserve The Father God Gave Them

Fatherless children are not only growing up without their fathers, but also without the support and love of the paternal relatives. It is virtually impossible for an excluded father to be a positive force in shaping the life of his child when intentionally kept away from his children.

Sociological studies confirm that children with an absent father are more disruptive in school, get lower grades, are more violent, commit more crimes, and twice as likely to have a drug problem as when a father is living in the home. Further studies show that 30% more children live below the poverty line when the father is absent. Children living in poverty, correspond almost exactly to the number of single-parent households.

Children are the real and ultimate victims of a divorce. Victims that very often end up in dead-end jobs, in gangs, in jails, or in cemeteries. The fatherless home is where the trouble starts. Children raised without the guidance of a father, get into more trouble, drop out of school, join gangs, live on welfare, and end up on the bottom rung of life.

Juvenile crime would be dramatically reduced if parental guidance of a father was kept intact. Jails are filling with children because of the missing dynamic in their lives, their father.

Solving the problem of fatherlessness will reduce crime rate dramatically and save the taxpayers billions of dollars. With such great rewards for the nation, it is incredible that government is not aggressively working toward solving the problem. Fathers must remain actively involved with their children, on a daily basis, as government does not have the economic resources to keep paying the price for this fatherless society.

Family lifestyles have changed dramatically in the past generation. Mothers are going to work every day just like fathers. Women have faced bias in the workplace in the struggle toward job equality, and men have the same uphill battle in the family law courts. You must accept that the family law court system is part of legal community that relies heavily on tradition, and the tradition is that mom raises the children.

Many sitting judges grew up in a traditional setting where they were raised by a mother. You are not going to change this perspective, learn to work within the parameters of the present legal system. The approach to the custodial decision is based on an impersonal, governmental function that is mother biased. A built in bias you need to accept, and contend with at every turn in the family law court system.

This overwhelming mom bias in the court system can only be fully appreciated by a father who has been through the wringer of a bitter custody battle. The day to day interaction with a child, and the opportunity to mold a life, is gone forever when the father becomes a weekend warrior.

The all-pervasive mom bias in family law court will change as society evolves to a gender-neutral legal system, new laws are enacted, and older judges retire. However, your children will be adults before the family law court system catches up with the societal changes of the past generation.

Mom bias in the legal system has been overcome by other fathers, and you can learn from their experiences. Your goal is to learn from their successes and use this book as a roadmap to guide you through the combat zone of a custody battle.

*CUSTODY FOR FATHERS* is your roadmap through a confusing legal system composed of a maze of technicalities. It unravels the mystery of the legal process, guides you through the judicial system, and teaches you what to do, and what not to do. This roadmap will help you through the tangling web of the family law courts, and show you how to overcome roadblocks, barriers, and obstacles. It will prepare you mentally for the long, emotional journey and teach you how to focus on your ultimate goal and final destination - Winning custody of your children.

Countless fathers have used the information in this book to successfully win custody of their children. There is a scarcity of published material on the issue of child custody. Educational materials on proper courtroom conduct, procedures, and etiquette are also not readily available, and what is in print, is hard to find.

This book, *CUSTODY FOR FATHERS*, was written to fill requests from the many fathers seeking information on the subject. The voices on the phone change, but the problems and issues are similar. Before now, fathers did not have a resource guide to use for consolidating problems, prioritizing issues, and packaging solutions. Hearing success stories about other fathers in like predicaments has given fathers options that might never have been considered. Carleen and I set aside three months of evenings and weekends to write this book, sat at the computer, shoulder to shoulder, and eleven months later our first edition was published. Work days we continue to run a busy law practice helping fathers with their unique problems. All of the strategies and tactics in this book are based on real life stories. The information gathered here took years to compile, and was derived from thousands of actual courtroom cases.

A courtroom is full of many hidden dangers and is not the place to experiment. The mental, emotional and financial cost of litigation can destroy a father. It is for this reason that some fathers abandon the fight altogether, throw in the towel, and walk. A father forced into taking such a position only results in a loss for the children. Don't go reinventing the wheel. Stick with what has worked for those fathers who have won custody. If a strategy has worked for another father, then consider using it in your own personal situation. Chart your own course by imitating what has worked for those fathers who have gone before you.

Reading this book demonstrates your sincere desire to take positive steps to win custody of your children and to preserve their well-being. Yet, desire alone is not enough. Winning a custody battle takes a good strategic plan. Start right now by building a strategy based on another fathers' techniques. Begin by reading the material we have provided herein, keep an open mind, and be willing to consider new alternatives. If something has worked well for another father, it can work for you.

This book is not intended to replace attorneys. There is no substitute for the experience and knowledge that an attorney can provide, as they have years of education and experience to draw upon. There is no guarantee as to the outcome of any legal action, and without the assistance of an experienced family law attorney, it is very difficult for a father to win custody. Fathers without an attorney should contact fathers rights groups, ask fathers who have won custody, and interview several experienced family law attorneys. Select an attorney who can quickly understand your personal situation, gives you sound advice, and offers positive solutions which are designed specifically for your case.

Engaging in a custody battle requires you to make serious financial commitments. The financial sacrifices you make today will be returned ten-fold in the future lives of your children. Find a way to finance your custody battle: Borrow money, arrange for a payment plan, barter your services, sell your possessions, do whatever it takes - your children's lives hang in the balance.

The greatest pleasure of your lifetime will be molding your children into upstanding, productive citizens. Begin right this moment to commit yourself toward making the sacrifices needed to win custody of your children.

This book cannot possibly substitute for competent legal advice. The law in each state will vary and the applicability of the law will depend on your individual circumstances. If you have a particular question about this book, please telephone us at our office, (949) 646-9842.

# CHAPTER 1

# WINNING

Action in court is fast, furious, and the stakes are high. Court orders have long-term serious consequences, and can turn lives upside down. You can recover mentally and emotionally from an act of nature: Hurricane, flood, fire, and famine, however, custody orders can cause human disasters from which you may never recover. You have absolutely no control over a natural disaster, but you do have control over your custody battle.

Winning a custody case is an art and not an exact science. You can win your custody battle if you commit to spending the time to adequately prepare your side of the case. This book is intended to give you the tools needed to build a winning strategy.

Many fathers become highly frustrated in their encounter with the family law system, it is new ground, and there are no roadmaps. Fathers find themselves involved in custody litigation with little or no courtroom experience, do not know how to conduct themselves, and have no place to turn for guidance. The difference between the winners and losers, is often technique.

In sports, the stadium is the field of battle, and in the legal system, a courtroom is your battlefield. Court is a non-contact sport, and gamesmanship revolves around words, actions, and body language. Both arenas are conducted with very strict rules. The players in sporting events understand and follow the rules, use them effectively, and execute established strategies to win. You would not even think of participating in a sporting event until after you learned the rules of the game. Likewise, you cannot expect to participate effectively in the legal system without learning how to strategize and conduct yourself in court.

## GAMESMANSHIP

Maneuvering within the rules is called, "gamesmanship," maneuvering outside the rules is called, "cheating." You do not want a judge to think you are cheating. Gamesmanship in athletics is often the difference between winning and losing. Acceptable gamesmanship in a sporting event are:

-       Basketball, intentional fouls to stop the clock.

-       Baseball, walking a batter to load the bases.

-       Football, long count to draw an offsides.

Judges and attorneys are trained in words, language, and behavior that are acceptable in court proceedings. They know when a violation has occurred, just as you know when a foul is made in a sporting event. Not every violation is called in either venue, sports or court. Most fathers entering the playing field of court, are not familiar with courtroom procedures, protocol, and rules. A father not knowing when a violation is being made in court is at a big disadvantage. This lack of knowledge of the procedures, protocol, and rules could cost him the game.

The judge is just like the referee in a sporting event. Trust in his/her wisdom and knowledge to know when the line has been crossed and a foul has occurred. Gamesmanship occurs in every case and judges know when it is going on and the motivation that is behind the tactic. Maneuvering within the rules of the game is smart. You will learn how to charm judges, mediators, and other court personnel, and how to outfox your opponent without doing anything illegal, immoral or unethical.

Wining strategies in court, just like in sports, involve the fair use of gamesmanship. Winning is an art that requires - thinking, planning, and implementing.

## THE GAME PLAN

You can win custody of your children by designing a game plan based on the winning strategies and techniques that have been successful for other fathers. The strategies and techniques outlined here are based on simple fundamentals. When used correctly, and at the right time, they are very effective and powerful. Learn to think like a family law judge and not as an impassioned litigant. You greatest weapon is: **Preparation, preparation, preparation.**

Maintain composure at all times as hasty decisions not well thought out, will only magnify problems, and get you into deeper trouble. You cannot afford to lose ground through impatient or reckless moves. Calculated, well-reasoned actions are what win custody battles.

Winning is often determined by the parent projecting the better image and giving the better presentation. Therefore, image and presentation must be prepackaged so all of the important information gets relayed to the family law judge. Judges base their orders on information provided in court testimony, as they have no prior knowledge of the facts. Judges are told lots of information in a very short period of time. For you to hear the magic words, CUSTODY TO FATHER, you must be prepared, organized, and ready on game day.

A winning game plan must be carefully developed, cleverly packaged, and precisely executed. Winning isn't easy. Winners make sacrifices. So, roll up your sleeves, start reading this book, and

never,

never,

never,

never,

**GIVE UP**

## CHAPTER 2

# THE FAMILY LAW SYSTEM

Family Law Court is where decisions regarding custody of your children will be made by a judge. Court is a confusing and complicated arena, where judges run their courtrooms differently from one another. The family law courthouse is where court forms, schedules, and procedures are constantly being modified in an almost futile attempt to streamline courtroom operations.

The family law courts operate in a way that can be strange, confusing, and frightening to newcomers. The complexity of the legal system is really only understood by a comparatively small group of litigating attorneys.

## UNDERSTANDABLE COMPARISON

To help you understand how the family law system works, we will be comparing it to the game of football. The game of football is a complicated business but can be easily understood by breaking the game down into individual elements. In much the same way, the legal system's complicated rules and information can be broken down into simple and easily understood elements. The rules in the game of football can be learned without knowing anything about other sports. Similarly, family law can be learned without knowing anything about other areas of law.

In football, a player must know certain things before he can effectively compete: For instance, 4 quarters to a game, 10 yards for a first down, 6 points for a touchdown, and so on. This analogy applies also to family law where you can effectively compete after informing yourself of things within the court system: Court mediation, master calendaring, the hearsay rule, and so forth. Football begins with one team being favored by a point spread. In custody battles, mothers are always heavily favored.

To win, the underdog team must go into the game with:

1)     Sound knowledge of opposing teams' weaknesses.
2)     A better game plan.
3)     Superior execution of that plan.

All fathers go into the custody battle as the underdogs. If you want to win, you must go into court with:

1)     Sound knowledge of opposing teams' weaknesses.
2)     A better game plan.
3)     Superior execution of that plan.

Upsets occur in football games, upsets occur in custody battles, and both upsets have similarities:

1) Sound knowledge of opposing teams' weaknesses.
2) A better game plan.
3) Superior execution of that plan.

We have repeated ourselves twice above to over stress the importance of preparation for fathers in uphill, family law custody battles. Your preparation will focus on the following areas which are outlined in great detail in this book:

KNOWLEDGE

PLANNING

EXECUTION

You learned the sport of football by playing in the park, practicing on a team, and watching games on television. This trial and error method is successful only if a lot of time is available. Years of learning allow for the trial and error approach to succeed. The stakes at risk in a custody battle do not afford you the time to flounder through a complicated process with which you have no knowledge. Therefore, the challenge ahead of you is much too important to leave to trial and error.

A father's preparation must exceed that of a mother to win a custody battle. This book will be your roadmap through the legal maze of a family law court system, and will empower you to avoid the pitfalls of the trial and error approach.

# THREE SIMPLE TERMS

To extract the relevant and pertinent information from the tremendous number of legal concepts involved in family law, we have developed three simple terms that will help you understand this very complicated area.

The following three terms and definitions here are used for this book only. These three terms are:

- *CODES*

- *RULES*

- *POLICIES*

These three terms, *Codes, rules, policies* provide you with some bite-sized portions of complicated legal concepts. We have used these three simple words, along with specific, definitions to distill the applicable legal concepts down into understandable, concise, and usable formats. Each term is defined separately on the following pages.

1.    **CODES**:

Codes refer to all state laws, and state laws cannot be changed by the judge. If your request is not according to codes, no matter how compelling it may be, the judge must deny your request.

**Example One:**
If you request change of custody after the divorce trial, you must show changed circumstances. The reason for this code is so the non-custodial parent cannot keep burdening the court with demands based on facts that are identical to facts brought before the court in the original trial.

**Example Two:**
All written documents, such as diaries, letters from doctors or teachers, school records, you want to show a judge come under the *Hearsay Rule.* The judge will make the decision whether any written documents will be accepted into the court record. The reasoning behind this code is to protect the court from easily falsified evidence.

*CODES:*    You cannot get a judge to do something contrary to codes . . . so don't ask.

## 2. *RULES:*

Rules refer to procedures followed by each local courthouse to help expedite the flow of cases. A judge can make exceptions to rules but only when the situation is extraordinary. Too many requests for exceptions to the rules and the court system would break down.

**Example One:**
Your mediation appointment (where parents meet with a mediation counselor at the courthouse), is set according to the rules of your local court system, rules that only apply to that particular local courthouse. Judges have the authority to change, reset, or order further mediation.

**Example Two:**
If your case has already been heard by a specific judge, the court rules state that this judge has the authority to keep your case in front of him/her, rather than wasting another judge's time getting up to speed on the facts of your case.

*RULES:*  You very rarely can expect a deviation from the rules . . . so ask very cautiously.

## 3. POLICIES:

Policies refer to customary policies of an individual judge when he/she is presented with a request. Occasionally judges will make exceptions to their policies, but only when they feel the request is valid, sincere, and supportive of justice.

**Example One:**
Children often want to give their opinion to the judge about where they want to live. The policy of each individual judge will decide whether or not the children will have the opportunity to give their preference.

**Example Two:**
You may want to use an outside psychiatric evaluator's services to confirm your allegations of physical or mental abuse. Each individual judge has his/her own policy of when such an evaluation should be made.

*POLICIES:* You often can get a judge to deviate from his policies . . . so ask, but respectfully, and be sure to have a detailed explanation.

## OVERVIEW OF TERMS

Knowing these three terms along with the definitions and examples will allow you to assess your problems and then decide which strategy you will use.

Let's review the terms one more time:

*CODES:*  You cannot get a judge to do something contrary to codes . . . so don't ask.

*RULES:*  You very rarely can expect a deviation from the rules . . . so ask very cautiously.

*POLICIES:*  You often can get a judge to deviate from his policies . . . so ask, but respectfully, and be sure to have a detailed explanation.

Since you have successfully journeyed through this broken field of legalese. The rest of this book will rely on your common sense and people sense. Way to go! You have just completed the hardest part of this book. Learning legal terminology (legalese) is like learning a foreign language without a dictionary.

## LEGALESE CAN OVERWHELM

You cannot expect to cram three years of law school into a frantic weekend in your county law library. You will find yourself faced with literally thousands of books with millions of pages. It would be a miracle for you to even locate the legal references relevant to your situation.

Even if you manage to locate applicable statutes and cases on point regarding your particular situation, you would still need to interweave the specific elements of your factual situation with the generalizations and dated results of your legal research. Then, you would need to attempt interpretation of these findings.

A law library is a very confusing place. Your trip there will be a waste of your time and therefore, counterproductive if you are unable to locate the legal information that is being sought. Your efforts are better spent reading this book than trying to teach yourself the law.

Legal research is best left to the experienced family law attorney. Concentrate your energies on more productive pursuits which are the proper use of wording, body language, and actions. Your time will be better spent learning about your local court system and how to conduct yourself in a courtroom. Learning how your local courthouse operates is explained fully in the next chapter.

## CHAPTER 3

# LEARN YOUR COURTHOUSE

There are thousands of Family Law Courts in America. Each imposes certain procedural guidelines that must be followed, and operates completely differently from the others. In California, there are 58 separate county courts and many have satellite courts. Each individual courthouse has its own method of moving paperwork and people through its system. Procedural changes are constantly being implemented in an attempt to streamline an overloaded court system. Therefore, your experiences in the legal system will be different from another father.

Do not worry about the procedural technicalities of your courthouse, as the strategies in this book work successfully with any court system.

Courthouses are overburdened with massive caseloads, chronic staff shortages, and grave security problems. Family law courts are the busiest of all courtrooms. Many family law courts have calendars with over 100 cases per day, and might have only three judges available to handle the caseload.

Fifty (50%) of first marriages and Seventy (70%) of second marriages end in divorce. The high number of divorces has caused an over congested court system that cannot adequately address each individual problem. Divorces involving a custody battle are an extra burden on the court system, because of the need for additional court staff such as mediators, counselors, and mental health professionals.

The increased number of divorces, most having custody disputes, has caused each courthouse to devise a unique system to keep the huge caseload moving. Accordingly, your courthouse will constantly be implementing new changes designed to move cases through the system more rapidly and efficiently. Because of these ongoing changes, you must go to your local courthouse and learn firsthand how your court system works.

The way to inform yourself about your local courthouse and how it operates, is to take a fieldtrip. Learning the actual physical layout of the courthouse building and the location of the departments before your own court date, will be very beneficial. By orienting yourself to the building, you will be on time, know where to go, and not be disoriented or frazzled when your own court date arrives. Court clerks can be of great assistance in helping with the procedural maze of your local court system. Be pleasant, courteous, and polite. Don't be afraid to ask questions.

## FIELDTRIPS TO THE COURTHOUSE

In football, the stadiums are different in each city, but the playing field is exactly the same. In family law, the courthouses are different, but the human problems are exactly the same. Make several fieldtrips to your local courthouse. Learn from real life family law cases by watching how strategies are effectuated. Football players watch other games as a learning experience, you must do likewise. Learn by observation.

Your fieldtrip will help you prepare for your own day in court. Sit quietly in the courtroom when watching a custody battle in progress. Observe the interaction of attorneys, litigants, judge, and courtroom staff. Pay attention to what irritates the individual judge, the demeanor of the litigants, and body language between the staff. You will learn the rhythm and pattern of how cases are conducted in your local courthouse. You cannot rely on another father's interpretation of how the court system works because his information might be outdated. Visit your local courthouse.

The rules for each courthouse can be obtained by getting a copy of the booklet entitled, **Local Rules** that is available in your local county law library. The clerk of the court's office has additional pamphlets that will be helpful.


## PIECES TO THE PUZZLE

1.  **The Facilities:** Check out the location of the parking, restrooms, telephones, photocopiers, and the family law courtrooms. Knowing these locations ahead of time, will reduce your stress level when your day in court arrives.

2. **The Clerk's Office:** The clerk's office is where you can readily obtain pamphlets, flyers, and notices about the courthouse rules. This is also where fees are collected, documents are filed, and stamped. Court clerks will refer to a stamped-returned copy of court documents as a *Conformed Copy.*

3. **The Forms Window:** This is where you can pick up preprinted court forms called, *Judicial Council Forms.* While you are at the form's window, pick up a brochure listing all the forms available so you can begin familiarizing yourself with court terminology.

4. **The File Room:** Your case-file can be reviewed with proper photo identification. Photocopies can be obtained, but are expensive, sometimes as high as $1.00 per page. You can also review the clerk's notes about your court hearing, on a preprinted form called a *Minute Order.* A photocopy with the court seal affixed is called a *Certified Copy* and is needed by police for enforcement.

5. **The Mediation Office:** This is where you will meet with a court appointed counselor, along with the mother of your children, in an attempt to come to an agreement for a parenting plan. *Mediation* is conducted according to the rules of your local courthouse. Mediation procedures can vary from courthouse to courthouse as they are conducted according to local rules - the differences can be dramatic.

Many courthouses have metal detectors similar to those at an airport. Leave any metal objects at home such as: Nail clippers, pocket knives, scissors, etc. A security guard will not allow such items into the courthouse. Anyone with a potentially dangerous item will be closely monitored.

## CUSTODY STAYS IN ONE COURT

After a divorce or paternity action has been filed in one court, the custody issue stays in that court even if modifications are sought years later. A custody issue can be changed to another county or state jurisdiction when both parents have moved away from the original court. When this happens, the case is moved to the court closest to children's residence. The reasons for selecting the court nearest the children are that court staff is better able to verify living conditions, check on school records, obtain witness statements, and other necessary information.

The custody issue is decided by a family law judge in the county where the parents reside. Some mothers intentionally flee the jurisdiction of the local court and file for custody thousands of miles away. This flight is often motivated by an attempt to avoid facing local witnesses who could testify against her, or to keep the father from having contact with his children. It is very difficult and expensive for a father to fight an out-of-state custody battle.

Each state has a different time period for establishing residency, and often jurisdiction is critical to the custody issue. If mom leaves the area with your children, then file court papers immediately as this will give jurisdiction to your local courthouse. There is a definite advantage to having local witnesses available to testify in court for you.

**Example:** Assume mom tells dad she is taking the children to relatives to "sort things out," and her secret reason is to establish residency and file for divorce in another court. If dad knew mom's real purpose for leaving the area was to establish jurisdiction elsewhere, he would be better off filing first, so that the custody battle would be held locally.

# COURTROOM SPECIALIZATION

Your local county courthouse is divided into separate courtrooms and each of these courtrooms is responsible for the handling of specific problem areas:

Juvenile     -     Teenagers

Criminal     -     For Crimes

Probate     -     For Death

Family Law     -     For Divorce/Custody

Courtroom specialization allows the judge and courthouse staff to become very knowledgeable in these specialized areas of the law. Each of these problem areas is covered by highly technical codes. Family law judges hear similar situations day after day and develop individual policies for dealing with repetitive problems.

When taking a fieldtrip to your local courthouse, visit all of the family law courtrooms. You want to familiarize yourself with the personalities of the different family law judges. Watch how each judge conducts hearings and controls his/her courtroom. Listening to other cases will give you insight into each individual judge's thought process. If you stay long enough in the courtroom, you will see the same problems coming up over and over again. You will also begin to know each judge's individual policies when he/she is presented with the same problems. The worst scenario is for a judge is to misidentify a problem, place a father in the wrong "pigeonhole," and apply an incorrect solution.

Fieldtrips to the courthouse will give you an opportunity to observe courtroom dynamics, drama, and tension. You will see firsthand how judges must interpret truthfulness or untruthfulness of a witness by:

- Demeanor and mannerism.

- Firmness and conviction in voice.

- Attitude toward court proceedings.

- Inconsistent statements.

While you are observing courtroom proceedings, conduct yourself as a responsible and mature adult. Judges and courtroom personnel remember disrespectful persons. Improper behavior will reflect immaturity. Be mindful that any misconduct in the courthouse, hallways, or parking lot will be noted and reported back to the judge. Video cameras cover all courthouse grounds.

Highly charged emotions are expected and anticipated in family law courts. Bailiffs in family law court, see more action in a month, than jail bailiffs do in a year. Fathers that get caught up in shouting, swearing, name-calling, pushing, shoving, slamming doors, and any other disruptive behavior, will be categorized as unstable, and perceived not a good role model for their children.

Family law personnel think they have seen and heard it all in the area of family breakups. It is your responsibility to project yourself as a mature individual who would be an excellent role model for children. Act appropriately when faced with adversity so your true character shines through.

# CALENDARING FORMAT

While you are investigating your local Family Law Court, learn how it apportions out the caseloads to the judges. To do this, go to the clerk's office and ask whether your court uses:

## *Judge For All Purposes Format*

or

## *Master Calendaring Format*

There is a distinct difference in how cases are handled with each of these two formats. You will apply a different strategy depending on which format is used by your local courthouse. Both formats are meant to move cases expeditiously through the legal system, but there are strategic moves that can be used with one format and not the other. An explanation and analysis of each calendaring format will prepare you for either system.

### *Judge For All Purposes Format:*

Judge For All Purposes Format is the procedure used by courts that assign your case to a specific judge for all purposes. The assignment of a specific judge is made when a case is initially filed, and usually according to the last digit on the case number. The judge in the department assigned, will hear all of a case from start to finish.

Judges in family law deal with large volumes of cases and do not have time to know each person. However, judges do get to know those parents who are repeatedly in court.

A judge hearing a case from beginning to end, will decide early on which parent is being more difficult. So, do not lose your temper nor act irrational in court with a judge whom you will be seeing you again and again. Judges using this type of calendaring format are generally assigned cases in the following way.

**Example:**

Judge A gets cases ending with digits   0, 1, 2, 3

Judge B gets cases ending with digits   4, 5, 6

Judge C gets cases ending with digits   7, 8, 9

After observing the family law judges in your courthouse, and make the determination that a particular judge would be good for your case, consider filing first to get the judge you want. Knowing the digits assigned to a specific judge will mean you might have to stand in line and let people go ahead of you, until you get the desired judge.

*Master Calendaring Format:*

Master Calendaring Format is the procedure used to assign the day's caseload among the judges. A list of the day's cases is posted outside the master calendar courtroom. The master calendar judge will call out each case, ask for a time estimate, and then send the cases to other judges according to the time estimates given at the calendar call.

With this Master Calendaring Format it is very likely that different judges will hear different parts of your case as you go back to court on other appearances. Attorneys maneuver their cases according to policies of individual judges. This format encourages attorney gamesmanship as attorneys try to avoid certain judges in order to get their cases assigned to more favorable judges.

## MORNING ACTION

The time for you to observe family law cases is early in the morning as this is when all parties are directed to appear. Plan on staying until noon. The experience and knowledge obtained is worth taking a half day off from work.

Those fathers that take the time to study the workings of their local courthouse, will have an advantage when it comes time to applying strategies and tactics. The clerks and bailiffs can be a valuable source of information. The more you know about your own local courthouse and how it works, the more prepared you will be for your day in court.

# CHAPTER 4

# BASIC STRATEGIES
# &
# TACTICS

The cardinal rule for winning, which applies not only to sports but also in careers, and all other endeavors, including your custody battle, is:

Practice - Practice - Practice
of
FUNDAMENTALS

Only after mastering basic fundamentals of a sport can you expect to participate in a game situation and develop a strategy. This analogy also holds true for your court situation.

There are training camps for sports, with veteran coaches, that are providing the necessary instruction needed to become a professional athlete. Because of these training camps, the basic strategies and tactics for professional athletes have already been worked out by experts. There are no such training camps available for fathers preparing for a custody battle, and resource materials are virtually nonexistent. Fathers entrenched in a brutal custody battle, are at a very stressful period in their lives, and are not in a mental frame of mind to be thinking clearly. Therefore, this is not the time for a father to be experimental. Follow what other fathers have done before. Do not try to reinvent the wheel.

## FUNDAMENTALS

Winning requires you to practice some basic fundamentals repeatedly. You need to react instinctively to situations without having to think through complicated options just like professional athletes do when it comes time to compete in the game.

Basketball......shooting, dribbling, jumping

Football...........blocking, tackling, kicking

Tennis..............serving, rallying, volleying

Golf.................driving, chipping, putting

These oversimplified examples of basic fundamentals in sporting events are meant to reinforce rules of basic fundamentals. Practice, hard work, and attention to detail are what will separate winners from losers. Practicing the fundamentals is monotonous, time consuming, and hard work, but the price one pays to win.

## MINOR ERRORS LOSE GAMES

In a sporting event, a few minor errors can make the difference between winning and losing. The same holds true in a courtroom. One small mistake might be the deciding factor. Your strategy is to "stay on your toes" mentally so that if you make a mistake, you can quickly apply the appropriate damage control measures.

You need to instinctively perform basic fundamentals, so your actions become second nature. Your mind should be free to concentrate on strategizing your moves, rather than worrying about compliance with technicalities.

For every offensive play in sports, there is a correct defensive counter play. In courtroom proceeding, it is exactly the same:

Correct **offensive** maneuvers

and

Correct **defensive** maneuvers

An experienced athlete sees a play developing and will instinctively go into action without consciously thinking through the different possibilities. Constant practicing of fundamentals pays off for an athlete when he knows exactly how to react in a given situation. You can train yourself to respond similarly in the courtroom by reading thoroughly the materials provided herein, and completing the exercises as outlined.

The basic strategies and tactics outlined here, have been developed from many years of experience and observation in the family law courts. They are the common thread that runs through those cases where fathers have won custody. These strategies and tactics have been tested and proven in previous cases, and are the strategies and tactics common to winning fathers.

**Preparation:** Study, rehearse, memorize, and implement those strategies that have worked for other fathers. Once again, don't try to reinvent the wheel. The stakes cannot get any higher than those in family law court. You cannot expect to win if you try to develop new strategies through trial and error. Commit to the time and effort necessary and prepare as if lives are at stake - they just might be.

To set in motion preparation for those strategies that have worked for other fathers you must:


**STUDY**

**REHEARSE**

**MEMORIZE**

**IMPLEMENT**


Being prepared will help you to overcome obstacles that will come up during your custody battle. Being prepared will also help you maintain your composure and gain self-confidence.

## 1.    SOUND APPEARANCE

Appearing physically, mentally, and emotionally sound in court seems so basic, yet, fathers don't think about the importance of appearing grounded and emotionally sound when facing a court hearing. We have seen countless fathers lose in court because they did not present themselves well, and came across as unsound, while other fathers that appeared to be sound - won.

Watching court hearings, will give you the opportunity to observe, get a feel for the judges personality traits, and see what kinds of arguments are working and what kinds are not working. Seeing first hand how people handle themselves in a court hearing will be a definite eye-opener. The time spent observing other cases will also give you a chance to get over natural nervousness, and give you a little more time to position yourself.

The decisions made by a judge can turn your life upside down, and you want to make a good first impression. You want to come across as a sincere person, someone that is truthful, even when it hurts. The judge is used to hearing from parents that give facts in a favorable light and always seem to have someone else to blame. This may require admitting past mistakes in order to be believed by a judge. A judge's job is made much easier once he/she believes the true facts have been given. Your first appearance in front of a judge will set the impression level.

Consider yourself being observed from the time you pull into the courthouse parking lot until after you leave. People are looking out of windows, video cameras are everywhere, and there are undercover officers around. Keep your conduct and behavior in check at all times.

## 2.    NO WHINING:

Staying focused will be one of your hardest assignments. There are going to be emotional factors that will fragment your thinking and upset you. However, it is very important to always project a positive attitude no matter how terrible you feel inside.

Whining, and complaining only makes you appear unstable and not mature enough to raise children, maybe even considered a "nut case." Your actions in and around the courthouse will be observed closely and immature conduct will be reported to the judge. Remember, there are video cameras hidden everywhere; in the hallways, restrooms, and parking lots. Winning fathers do not waste their time complaining about inequalities of the legal system.

Judges hear fathers' complain daily about courts:

-        Favoring mothers.

-        Treating fathers unfairly.

-        Ignoring the children's wishes.

Do not waste your valuable courtroom time on arguments that will not help your case. You are not going to change how the courts and legal system operate, and such complaints only makes you appear ungrounded. Save your legitimate complaints about the inequalities of the legal system until after your individual case is over. Only when you are finished with your case can you work toward making changes in the legal system.

### 3.    PHYSICAL, MENTAL, EMOTIONAL READINESS

Physical, mental, and emotional well-being are expected of a father that wants to raise his children. Yet, it is expected for a mother to be a bit out of sorts during a custody battle. There is definitely a male and female double standard in a court hearing when it comes to emotions displayed. Knowing about this double standard ahead of time, will help you learn to work with it rather than to fight it.

### Physical Readiness

Physical readiness means looking healthy and fit. Think about going to a tanning salon, as having a ruddy complexion is often considered the sign of a person with an alcohol problem. Do a little bit of exercise every day, even if it's just a 20 minute walk, it will give color to your skin tone.

Judges like to see a father with a lifestyle that is stable; one that involves his children in many grounded activities, hobbies, church attendance, and regular daily schedules. This projects a well-balanced father who will teach similar traits to his children. Such a father will be looked upon as one who enjoys spending time with his children.

A judge wants to feel that a father will serve as a positive role model for his children. This image is projected through your conduct, attitude and behavior. Physical appearance and good grooming are essential. Remember, you never get a second chance to make a first good impression. You must be clean shaven, with combed hair, pressed shirt, pants, and wear socks.

## Mental Readiness

Being mentally ready is necessary in order for you to think clearly when in court. Your mental stability will be displayed by having a clear head.

This requires you to abstain from alcohol, illegal drugs, or any other kind of medication that will affect your alertness. Courts will test for alcohol and drugs when mom makes an allegation. Testing can be done as early as the first session with the mediation counselor, and this testing can continue randomly. Any missed test will be considered a "dirty test."

## Emotional Readiness

Emotional readiness means you can control yourself when in a stressful situation. Temper outbursts will be seen as immature conduct and considered a sign of an unstable person. The inability to control your emotions, in the courtroom, will suggest you are probably worse at home.

Many custody wars involve a mom and dad that do not speak to one other. If you are in this situation, do not use your time at the courthouse to try and discuss problems with mom. Trying to engage mom in a conversation can too easily mark you as a "dumpee." If you cannot communicate with mom without an argument, get help from a relative or friend. Routing messages through law offices gets very expensive.

Maintaining your composure and staying in control shows you can handle difficult situations. This demeanor will project emotional stability.

## 4.    GET OUT OF THE LEGAL SYSTEM FAST:

As a rule, fathers that have won custody usually get what they want early on, and get out of the legal system quickly and quietly. This can prove quite difficult when there is a vindictive mom on the other end that does not want to accept reality and keeps up a constant flow of court hearings. When mom keeps dad stuck in the legal system with continuous, never-ending litigation, a father must stop and rethink his strategy to get unstuck.

Those fathers that do not get through the legal system fast, generally, do not do well. The ever-present mom bias eventually catches up and weighs down on those fathers stuck in continual litigation. Therefore, be willing to compromise on minor issues so you can get out of the system quickly and successfully. Constant haggling over small things will keep you stuck, make you look petty, and can have disastrous results.

> **Note:** The longer a father stays in the legal system, the greater his chances of losing. This basic tactic of getting through the legal system fast should be a primary goal. Strategize early, set the pace, and be willing to concede on peripheral matters.

Cases that get stalled in the system result in continuous court appearances, skyrocketing costs, and any progress made comes to a screeching halt. The pervasive mom bias of the legal system will catch up with you and pulverize you. If you win your major points get out of the courthouse building, FAST. Sticking around to win every little point allows the judge to rethink those major points while you are arguing over the minor points.

A good strategy is not to be the first case heard on court day. Like every other person, judges have their off days. If a judge is being difficult on a particular day, then you want to tread softly and learn what annoyances are setting off the judge. While you are awaiting your turn, be polite and display respectful body language. Use this extra court time to mentally prepare and rehearse your presentation to the judge. Watch the judge closely and see what works. If a person's strategy or tactic has failed, then avoid using it yourself.

As the lunch hour approaches, parents will begin making concessions to avoid coming back in the afternoon. Just before the noon break is an excellent time to settle issues. Opportunity knocks for the fathers that are alert. After the lunch hour, parents tend to come back strong, refreshed, and rejuvenated from the noon meal, and there is a resurgence of hostilities and anger. Judges know that when parents have spent all morning in court without resolving the issues, it is very likely that one parent is being obstinate.

Should you spend the morning in fruitless negotiations, and be required to return after the lunchtime, it is a good strategy to come back into the courtroom appearing friendly, smiling a lot, and projecting a non-difficult personality. The judge will be looking for body language from both parents that will indicate which one is causing the negotiations to go nowhere.

**Note:** Hanging the "difficult" sign around the neck of mom by your being cheerful and agreeable, will convey to the judge that mom is the stubborn one.

## 5. WHEN YOU GET STUCK - STOP EVERYTHING:

When you find yourself stuck - stop everything. Admit to yourself when you are "stuck," as it is essential to your getting "unstuck."

Being stuck in the legal system is defined as:

- Finding yourself with continuous and endless court appearances.

- Negotiations are going nowhere and are therefore, fruitless and time wasting.

- Your reasonable compromise offers are being flatly refused.

- Stupid and bizarre allegations are being made.

- Your checkbook balance is a good indicator of just how bad you are stuck.

The legal system is like a minefield, and your straying off the proven path, will only result in explosions. Give yourself the time needed to reevaluate your situation. An experienced soldier stuck in a minefield will stop all movement, reevaluate, and then proceed cautiously on a new course. A stuck litigant should do likewise. When stuck in litigation, stop everything, analyze your present situation, and begin designing a new approach for your particular case.

Once you are mentally at a full stop, think through past events, and examine the mistakes that have led up to the present situation. Consider how differently things might be if you had taken a different course of action. Reflecting back over the past occurrences will allow you to think through alternate ways to deal with problems.

Any changes in your strategy need to be thoroughly analyzed and well thought out. Hasty moves generally result in mistakes that will get you deeper in trouble and make it harder to get back on track. Custody battles require strategies and tactics that are well-reasoned, well-executed, and only modified after very careful deliberation.

Heed the words of the world renowned genius, Albert Einstein:

*"I think and think for months and years Ninety-nine times the conclusion is false - The hundredth time I am right."*

Looking at problems from a different angle will help you gain new perspective and by that allow you to consider alternative solutions.

Einstein's theory for solving problems:

*"You cannot extricate yourself from a problem, by using the same thought process that got you into the problem"*

Einstein was right about all his other theories. And, they revolutionized the way we live today. Follow his advice.

## 6.    CHANGE YOUR THOUGHT PROCESS:

The problems you have encountered with your court case, can be turned around, BUT only by changing your present thought process. Start by accepting Einstein's theory of problem solving, and then begin changing your thought process. It is mandatory you to commit to a completely new way of thinking, analyzing, and reasoning.

So let's begin by:

-         Isolating key issues.

-         Weighing alternative solutions.

-         Learning different techniques.

-         Considering new ideas.

-         Launching a fresh approach.

Start changing your habits and routines. Making changes in old patterns will force you to be more mentally alert, and open to new options. The more changes you make in your set ways, the more open you will be to seeking alternative solutions, different techniques, fresh ideas and varied approaches.

Changing ones thought process is not an easy task. You are already programmed and have trained your mind to respond in a certain way, so it will take a major effort on your part to think and act in a different way. Taking a brisk walk daily will release endomorphic enzymes in the brain cells and activate your thought process.

Here are other simple, everyday changes you can make:

- If you always drive in the fast lane, change to the slow lane.

- If you take a specific route to work, change your route and see new sights.

- If you watch a lot of television, switch to reading more newspapers, magazines or books.

- If you shop at a particular store, change stores and meet new clerks.

- If you routinely eat hamburgers, then switch to pasta.

Training yourself to develop a new thought process will be a constant struggle. Old habits and routines are second nature and are done without conscious thinking. Making small changes in your day-to-day life will help you make the bigger changes in the way you approach problem solving.

**Note:** A square peg won't fit in a round hole, and repeated attempts are futile and draining. Change your thinking by backing off from the dilemma and taking a new approach. A poker player who changes technique in the midst of a card game, throws off opponents, and gains a significant advantage.

## 7. AVOID COMMON BLUNDERS:

Strategies and tactics must accentuate your strengths and exploit mom's weaknesses as you do not want to expend energy on correcting mistakes and going on wild goose chases. You need to come across as a mature individual so that you will be classified as a father capable of doing a terrific job of raising children.

There is a double standard for males and females as to conduct, and this gender conduct is perceived differently by a judge. Females can get away with displaying immature conduct, because these hysterical females are seen as over protecting their children. Conversely, males exhibiting this kind of behavior are considered very dangerous. Thus, fathers are held to a higher maturity level. Accept this double standard as a reality, knowing other fathers before you have faced this fact and overcome it. **You can too.**

If a female acts in an immature manner by leaving strange phone messages, writing bizarre notes, and acting abnormally, she will not be viewed as a potentially violent person. Yet, if a male acts immaturely and irrationally, he will be considered as a serious threat.

One careless misstep by a father can overturn a lifetime of good deeds. So, think carefully before leaving phone messages, sending notes, showing up unexpectedly, calling mom's workplace, or creating a scene. Before you do anything, get opinions from people you respect, friends, or relatives, and then consult with your attorney.

### You Cannot Afford To Make A Mistake!!!

Some of the most common blunders to avoid are:

**DO NOT:** Leave offensive messages on mom's answering machine.

**DO NOT:** Make frequent phone calls to mom's work.

**DO NOT:** Create a scene in front of family, friends or children.

**DO NOT:** Spread gossip about mom, as it will come back on you.

**DO NOT:** Use your children as a go between for spying.

On the other hand:

**DO:** Document pertinent events with a diary, take photographs, and make tape recordings.

**DO:** Assemble school records in an easy to read booklet.

**DO:** Identify and use any reliable, unbiased witnesses.

**DO:** Consult with a mental health professional who will help you.

**DO:** Keep the best interest of your children in mind at all times.

## 8. RECORD YOUR STRENGTHS:

To convince a judge that you should be the custodial parent you will need to:

Put together a binder that emphasizes all of your positive character traits. It can include the following: Diplomas, certificates, letters, awards and any other writings proving your character. A judge will not examine each writing, but will be impressed by your effort.

Write down all your honorable qualities and significant accomplishments - things that show maturity. Make it brief, concise, and formatted like a resume. Have the list typed for easy reading.

Let the judge know that you encourage your children to attend church regularly, develop good study habits, participate in extracurricular activities, and enjoy healthy relationships with ALL relatives.

All these efforts will demonstrate your parenting skills and show your ability to be a good role model for your children. You want the judge to know that your main concern, as a father, is for the well-being of your children. Putting together a portfolio shows commitment, effort, and dedication on your part in seeking custody of your children.

## 9. EXPLOIT MOM'S WEAKNESSES:

Mom's weaknesses need to be accurately brought before the court, but must be dealt with very delicately, and in a way that does not make you appear vengeful. If your intent is interpreted as being spiteful when revealing a mom problem, your revelations might be viewed as motivated by revenge. You want to expose mom's weaknesses, but in a way that does not appear you are trying to embarrass.

After informing the judge of mom's problem areas, he/she will want to know how you handled her negative behavior while living with her. In other words, if there was such a big problem, what did you do about it. If you did nothing about it, why not. Your not doing anything about her problem, might be interpreted as being more harmful than the actual problem itself. You must keep good records.

**Calendar:** Purchase a calendar or diary from a stationary store and record mom's behavior. If you can, document with photographs, as you will be more believable if your version of events is supported by accurate records.

**Reports:** Any reports being given in court, should be offered in a reserved fashion so that a spiteful motivation by dad is not implied.

A judge will scrutinize every piece of evidence offered. If you are forced to report bad things about mom, make sure you do not look as if you are enjoying yourself.

## 10. GET CHILD SUPPORT FROM MOM:

It is very common for fathers who have been awarded custody to waive child support from mom. Waiving child support might be well intended, however, it can backfire on you if mom comes back to court later, seeking custody. A main concern of a judge hearing a post-judgment request from a non-custodial parent for custody is, if child support payments have been regular and kept up-to-date. It is difficult for a mom that has not paid child support to convince a judge that she is a proper parent.

A child support order serves as a barrier that mom must overcome before taking dad back into court for switch of custody. A dad not asking for child support, leaves mom in the position of not having anything to lose if she decides to take dad back into court seeking custody.

Unpaid child support, no matter how small, will add up over time, and interest will accrue. The monies are for the benefit of the children and will be collected free of charge by the District Attorney's Office in your county. The money can be held in a trust account for future use: Children's education, down payment on a home, or establishing a career.

Child support is only accrued if there is a Court Order. If mom's whereabouts are unknown, you can still obtain a Court Order for child support. Mom can be found through governmental agencies and when found, her wages will be garnished. Hunting down a delinquent parent should not be thought of as vengeful in nature, because the money is rightfully due to enhance the lives of your children.

## 11.  KEEP GOOD RECORDS:

Any documents you want presented to the judge such as: Diaries, photographs, notes, letters, police reports, etc., should be cataloged and indexed in a binder with a table of contents for quick reference.

Sometimes, a diary is the most critical piece of evidence because of its accuracy in recalling dates, times and the location of events. Writings come under the *Hearsay Rule*, and some writings may not be admitted into evidence by the judge because concern arises as to whether the writing was made at the time of the event. Judges will use the word "contemporaneous."

**Diary:** Often, the most crucial piece of evidence is a diary. A diary is used to refresh a person's recollection of dates, times, locations of events, and generally does not come into evidence as a complete manuscript. When being asked questions during your testimony, use your diary to recall specific and exact events.

**Writings:** Any writings offered into evidence should be kept short so they will be read. Written notes are very useful when you need to convince a judge that your version of events is a more accurate rendition than moms. Short summaries of events on a single calendar or diary, written at the time of occurrence, will also be very persuasive to a judge. The judge may not review each document, but he/she will be aware that you are not just "winging it," as your version is based on notes taken at the actual time of the events.

**Photographs:** Photographs can be an excellent way to present evidence to a judge if he/she believes that the photographs are true representations of what they show. A judge flips through them very quickly but will get a good idea of what you are trying to convey. A judge will require the person who took the photos to testify in court as to their authenticity. Therefore, if at all possible, take the photographs yourself.

**Video And/Or Tape Recordings:** Videos are difficult to use as you need to have a TV/VCR. Also, it is necessary to use court time for the setting up of a video and this is distressing to some judges. Tape recordings you want the judge to hear will have similar logistical complications.

**Colored Flip Charts:** Colored flip charts can be effective if done in a neat, clear, and informative manner. The flip charts are most frequently used to depict time periods with the children.

**Note:** Photographs, videos, charts, and/or tape recordings can be edited or altered to give a prejudicial point of view, and will be treated as such by the judge.

# SEX AND DRUGS

The two most volatile topics brought up in a family law court are:

## SEX

## DRUGS

These two subjects need to be addressed cautiously before they are reported to a judge. A judge only wants to hear testimony when the issue of sex or drugs is a real and current problem. The inflammatory nature of these two subjects is often brought up to shock a judge into taking action. Judges commonly see dads using these topics as a way to attack mom.

A dad testifying about moms immoral conduct must be careful not to appear spiteful or vengeful. If you need to bring up misconduct by mom to the judge, be very cautious in how this message is delivered. Attempting to prove mom is an unfit mother because of either sexual misconduct, or recent drug usage, must be presented in a way that does not make you look as though you are bent on revenge.

Mom's sexual adventures behind closed doors, and long past drug usage, will not be helpful to the judge when making the custodial decision unless it directly affects the children. If a judge interprets dad's reason for bringing up either of these subjects as pay back against mom, it will have a boomerang effect and be detrimental to his image.

## SEX

Sexual misconduct out of the children's presence, is not of concern to the judge. Judges do not want to hear about moms private sex life, unless it directly affects the children. And, it is very hard to prove that mom is having sex in front of the children without involving the children.

Involving the children in this area will only add to their trauma, and reflect poorly on your judgment. Telling a judge about mom's adultery, hyperactive sexual activity, or some other sexual misconduct might be interpreted as coming from a father whose intention is to humiliate or embarrass mom.

## DRUGS

Recent drug usage is a major concern to a judge and can be verified through blood testing. Bringing up long ago drug usage makes it look as if you are reaching for ancient "dirt," leaving one to believe that there are no recent drug problems. Both parents have a past, and old mistakes corrected have very little bearing on the present problems.

Many judges believe, that if one parent is doing drugs, so is the other parent. If not, what steps did the non-drug using parent take to remedy the problem situation.

Any witnesses who are going to testify about drug usage will be cautioned about the 5th Amendment, the potential for giving incriminating evidence, and the possibility of criminal charges being filed.

# POLICE REPORTS

Police reports are written documents made outside court, subject to the *Hearsay Rule*, and are not allowed into evidence. The hearsay rule applies because the police officer who wrote the report has no independent knowledge of what actually happened. A police officer cannot testify as an uninvolved third party witness.

People who chronically file police reports are under the impression that a large stack of paperwork will be influential and infer misconduct on the person being filed against. Police forms and log numbers do give some credibility to information on the police report filed, however a person who files multiple police reports, is often viewed as a vindictive person who is abusing police resources to manipulate the system.

Judges are well aware that any citizen can walk into a police station at any time, make a report, and then refer to the report as the official account of events. Usually these reports are slanted versions of actual happenings. If a police report has to be filed, use precautionary measures. If you can, take someone with you who can come to court and testify on your behalf to verify facts of actual events.

**Note:** Police officers do not have enough time for real and serious criminal problems, so frivolous reports are going to be considered a form of harassment. When making a police report, take along an unbiased witness who can verify the seriousness and correctness of your report.

# CONTEMPT

*Contempt* is a willful disobedience of a court order, and is an extremely complicated area of the law. Family law contempts are classified as civil, quasi-criminal because of the jail possibility, and the "contemner," having constitutional protection. A contempt conviction requires that four elements must be proven with sworn testimony. Think of this exercise as in baseball where the four bases must be touched, failure to prove any of the four elements results in a dismissal or a not guilty verdict.

| | |
|---|---|
| 1st Base: | Lawful court order. |
| 2nd Base: | Knowledge of the court order. |
| 3rd Base: | Ability to comply. |
| Home Plate: | Willful disobedience. |

A civil contempt is not an offense against the court, but against the party on whose behalf the court order was issued. Thus, in the family law setting, a contempt is actually brought by the opposing party and generally falls into two areas:

**1. Nonpayment of Support:** Contempt proceedings concentrate on ability of "citee" to make payments. No payment, or a fixed, reduced amount is a willful violation. A fluctuating payment based on ability to pay is more understandable for a reasonable doubt.

**2. Custody/Visitation:** A parent threatens the grounding of a teenager, knowing that the punishment is harder on the parent. Family law judges threaten moms with contempt, hoping a stern lecture will resolve the difficulties, knowing the hearing is hard to prove up. Work with the judge in the THREAT of jail time, as the constitutional safeguards over-protect the contemner.

# CRIMINAL ACTS

You cannot help your children when you are in jail. Be very careful in all of your actions and consider how your conduct will be viewed by a police officer hearing a different version of the story. You must not say or do anything that can be construed as a criminal act.

**Example:** If you follow mom to check on the safety of your children, this can be interpreted by a police officer as "stalking."

Custody battles are highly charged emotional experiences that often lead to criminal conduct. What starts out as a good idea, and innocent intention, can easily escalate into an out of control situation. If an argument leads to pushing and shoving, the female is always going to be considered the victim even when she is the aggressor. The way to win custody within the legal system, is to exercise patience, maintain composure, avoid confrontation, and prepare records that will influence all of the key players.

- The Mediators/Evaluators.

- The Unilateral Counselors.

- Ultimately, the Judge.

You must now begin preparing for you first stop in the system ... *mediation.*

# CHAPTER 5

# MEDIATION IN A NUTSHELL

The family law courts have developed a program called *Mediation* as the preferred way for "warring parents" to resolve custody/visitation problems of children without involvement of: Judges, attorneys, mental health professionals or social workers. Successful mediation avoids the need for psychiatric evaluations, homestudies, investigations and other personal affronts associated with government intrusions into your personal life.

Mediation is your last chance to resolve custody/visitation issues, without a judge making an order deciding the fate of your children. Judges want custody/visitation settled in mediation and get upset with a parent who does not cooperate.

# THE MEDIATOR'S ROLE

Mediators are professional counselors working for the court. They are trained to help parents work out a parenting plan. If parents do not come to a mutually agreed upon parenting timeshare plan, then the mediator will give parents the court's usual orders for similar type situations. The mediator does not deal with issues of child support, spousal support, property division, debt payments, or any other type of financial matters.

The only issues a mediator will discuss are those that deal with custody/visitation of the children. This includes areas of disagreement between parents, such as: telephone calls, school participation, extracurricular activities, transportation, and other areas of disagreement between parents. Complaints of alcohol or drug abuse are generally brought up during the mediation session. The mediator can request random drug testing of either parent any time, even at the first mediation session.

Once a mediator is assigned to a case, this mediator will stay with that case for the duration of employment with that courthouse. Therefore, it is in your best interest not to upset or antagonize your mediator. Instead, learn to work with this person. Mediators deal with all types of people from every walk of life, and try to find out which parent is better suited for raising the children. Your focus in mediation should be on persuading the mediator you are the better role model for your children. Let the mediator know your willingness to share the children with mom. "Shared parenting" is the key phrase to use in mediation.

Make notes ahead of time on the important facts you want to bring up in front of the mediator. You do not want to forget an important issue. You want the mediator to clearly understand all of the problems in your family situation.

# THE MEDIATION PROCESS

The mediation process is handled a bit differently in each courthouse. Variations in the process are intended to streamline and provide a more efficient way of moving the cases through the system. Fathers that know how their local mediation office works, how the cases are processed, and what is expected of them, will have a higher success rate than fathers that stumble through the system, learning by trial and error. Enter mediation knowing how your local system works, with alternative options reflecting your willingness to cooperate, and consider new suggestions.

There are operational differences in the various mediation offices with respect to information received from parents during the sessions. Find out how your local mediation works on one of your fieldtrips by asking questions of the receptionist.

Mediation can operate as follows:

- The mediator will make direct recommendations to the judge.

- The mediator submits a written evaluation of the case to the judge without a recommendation.

- The mediator is called to the witness stand, placed under oath, and testifies about the case.

- The mediator does not make a recommendation to the judge, and all discussions are confidential.

Judges have confidence in their court mediators. Judges realize mediators have more time than they do to delve into the personal lives of a family to verify allegations. Considerable time is spent by the mediator gathering up facts, verifying information, talking with children, and doing whatever it takes to accurately assess the family situation.

Each mediator establishes a reputation with judges by a personal track record based upon working together on prior cases. It is a statistical fact that judges follow the recommendations of mediators in 90% of all cases. Mediators giving unsound advice are replaced, so don't antagonize your assigned mediator.

After you have familiarized yourself with how your local mediation process works, you can begin preparing your 10-minute presentation. You will want to "role-play" your delivery with a friend. Talk with other dads who have recently been through mediation; you will find them in the waiting room, and at meetings of fathers rights groups. Discuss sensitive problems that might be brought up with family members and your attorney. The stakes are high. Give mediation your full attention.

Fathers that take the time to learn how their local court mediation process works, do much better than those fathers that just "wing" it. Knowledge of your local mediation process will be advantageous to you when sitting in front of a stranger/mediator who has fixed ideas and formula solutions for repetitive problems. Each individual mediator has a unique personal style and you want to learn it and play up to it. Knowing the individual style of your assigned mediator, lets you communicate on the same wavelength.

**Note:** Mediators are counselors and they all have common personality traits. Consult with someone who is in the counseling business for a practice session.

## STANDARD VISITATION GUIDELINES

Most mediation offices have formulated standard visitation schedules, which can be obtained at the mediation office, and are called, *Standard Visitation Guidelines*. Standard guidelines have been developed to accommodate visitation for the non-custodial parent according to children's ages. The guidelines might not make sense, but will give you an understanding of what your local court system has established as standard guidelines.

Visitation guidelines are available on preprinted forms. These forms are used to save time, so mediators do not have to waste time writing up the same schedule several times each day. Guidelines used by the mediation office are designed to fit the average family. There are many different family situations that require adjustments because of work schedules, time factors, and distance problems. Be prepared to discuss any adjustments needed because of individual circumstances with your family situation.

If the standard visitation guidelines need to be changed in your case because either parent: Works on weekends or evenings, travels for a living, resides far away, or any other extenuating circumstances, then adjustments can be made with the help of your mediator. Go to the mediation office and pick up a copy of the visitation schedules. Make desired changes on the visitation guideline form, as mediators are used to working with that specific form.

The more you know about your local visitation guidelines, the easier it will be to ask for changes because of your individual situation. Having a copy of the standard guidelines with changes you would like, makes the session easier on the mediator. Helping the mediator in such a manner will portray you as a father who has taken the time to offer positive solutions.

Read over the standard visitation schedules very carefully so you can be prepared to justify any changes you want to make. You want to thoroughly convince the mediator why you should spend more time with the children than is offered. Any reasonable requests will be considered on an individual basis.

The local guidelines are broken down into age bracket groupings similar to the following:

### Baby - Birth to 6 months:
Non-custodial parent should spend at least one or two hours with their baby at least three times a week.

### Infant - 6 months to 18 months:
Non-custodial parent should continue spending the one to two hour midweek periods with their infant child at least two or three times a week, and in addition, have the infant with them on weekends from Saturday 4:00 p.m. until Sunday 4:00 p.m.

### Preschool - 18 months to 6 years:
Non-custodial parent should continue spending the one to two hour midweek periods with their preschool age child at least two or three times a week. In addition, the non-custodial parent should have their preschool age child with them on the alternate weekends from Saturday 9:00 a.m. to Sunday 6:00 p.m.

### Children - 6 years to 12 years:

The non-custodial parent is allowed one telephone call per day. The non-custodial parent should have their child, one evening midweek up to four hours, and every other weekend from Friday evening until Sunday evening. Non-custodial parent is allowed one-half the summer, and alternating holidays. Christmas holiday is generally divided so that one parent gets their child from the close of school until noon Christmas day. The other parent gets noon Christmas day until school commences. Positions of the parents are reversed every other year.

### Teenagers - 13 years to 18 years:

The non-custodial parent shares less time with teenage children as they begin to demonstrate their independence. Teenagers will begin arranging their own social commitments, extracurricular activities, or start part-time jobs. This is when the judge will allow the children to decide how much time they want to spend with their non-custodial parent.

### SPECIAL DAYS:

Mothers' day with mother, Fathers' day with father, and each parent getting their birthday. Each parent shall spend equal time with their child on the child's birthday.

Familiarizing yourself with standard forms will help you to intelligently discuss your individual requests for variations that are different from the standard visitation guideline format.

Prevailing thinking holds that children of tender years should not be away from their mothers for long periods of time. The label for this is, *separation anxiety*. There is a strong belief held by many mediators that psychological trauma results in young children when they are separated from their mothers for an extended length of time, but not when separated from fathers.

Raising a child is not just a mother's responsibility, it is a father's too. When children grow up with little or no contact with a father, all of society suffers: School attendance declines, crime rates escalate, teenage pregnancies increase, and drug usage goes skyhigh. This continual dysfunctional family pattern continues and leads to another generation of fatherless children. Recycling of fatherless children only creates greater problems for all of us.

A child's greatest fear, at all ages, is separation from a parent. Frequent and sufficient contact with both parents would help overcome this childhood trauma. This childhood fear is exacerbated by a mobil population that relocates residences often. Parents divorce, move to different cities, and extended family members are no longer factored into the children's growth process. Standard visitation of every other weekend for the non-custodial parent means a child will go fourteen (14) days without contact with the non-custodial parent. A support column that the children are used to depending on every single day.

The most common wish of children who are going through a breakup of the family is that the parents get back together. This desire is fueled by the separation anxiety from the non-custodial parent, most commonly the father. Children are traumatized even further when they feel responsible for the breakup. Children want and need to spend lots of time with both parents.

# MEDIATION HELPS

Studies prove that children adjust better to their parent's separation if negative feelings are not displayed in front of the children. Hostilities are reduced when both parents can share equal time with their children. A successful mediation session avoids fighting, feuding, and resentments that can last for a lifetime.

Parents that reach a full agreement in mediation avoid:

- The bloodbath of a court hearing.
- Family confidences made public.
- Relatives forced to choose sides.
- Neighbor involvement.
- Embarrassment at work.
- Loss of longtime friendships.
- Disruption at children's school.

Parents that come to an agreement in mediation, have both made concessions for the benefit of the children. Give and take in mediation, resulting in a full agreement on parenting timeshare, may outweigh the damage caused to the children when "dirty laundry" is aired by either parent.

# TRADITIONAL MOM BIAS

Mediators and judges are "mom biased" because of the traditional thinking that only mothers can raise children properly. Mothers are assumed to be the better custodial parent due to some biological imprint. This thinking means fathers are only being considered for custody when mothers opt out because of prison, drugs, alcohol, mental instability, or some other type of deviant behavior.

The traditional thinking on the issue of custody results in mothers getting custody in 90% of custody battles. Mom bias is prevalent at every level of the family law system. Do not let the statistics discourage you, as you can learn to position yourself with those fathers that win custody. Your task is to study and use the strategies and tactics that have worked for the winning fathers.

Mom bias is a result of generations of mothers staying home and caring for the children, while dad was out working and providing for the family. It has only been one generation since mothers have left the house and joined the workforce. Many of today's judges grew up in an era of stay-at-home moms and this upbringing reflects in their thinking and decisions. This mom bias will change as the judiciary catches up with societal changes.

Today, it is essential for both parents to work just to make ends meet, and fathers are just as involved as mothers in caring for the children. Mediators and judges are aware of this evolution in the family unit, but realize the court system moves at a much slower pace and cannot keep up with a rapidly changing society.

The present attitude of judges and mediators in the family law court system is something you must learn to deal with. You are not about to alter traditional thinking that is firmly implanted in today's legal system. Save your energy for arguments you can win. Focus your attention on landing within the group of fathers that have won custody of their children. Attempting to change the legal system is a very worthwhile endeavor, but wait until you have completed your own custody battle. Radical attempts to change state laws while your case is pending, can make you appear too radical. Focus your energies on winning your own custody battle, and hold off changing the system until later.

# COUNSELING IS A FEMALE PROFESSION

The mental health profession consists mainly of women and the female mindset prevails whenever you find yourself in counseling situations. To be effective in such a setting, males must think like a woman. The typical male characteristics of problem solving are strong, silent, and assertiveness; all of which are counterproductive in a counseling session. You must let the counselor take the lead, adequately present your version of events, and let the counselor solve the problem.

Males are sometimes ineffective in counseling sessions due to miscommunication when they are not in sync with the female mindset. This female thought process will extend to the mediation sessions. Mediators will not change their thinking to fit your male psyche, so learn to make the mental adjustments to do well in mediation.

Linguistic studies have established that males and females are very different in the way they:

THINK
COMMUNICATE
REACT

It is mandatory for you to tailor your presentation so that your words will be effective in this female oriented mediation session. The next chapter expands on the exact terminology, intonation, and body language to use when in mediation. A major complaint of mediation by fathers is that they were not allowed to be fully heard. A father's frustration can be avoided by preparing short, concise versions of events that can be told without an interruption.

# COURT-APPOINTED EVALUATIONS

A judge in family law can appoint an independent evaluator (a professional mental health worker referred to as a *"forensic"* psychologist), when serious allegations are made about the safety of the children. The judge does not want to take the chance of making a mistake and leaving children at risk. The safer approach for a judge is to appoint a professional evaluator, someone who has the time necessary to personally interview neighbors, teachers, medical providers, significant others, and any other persons with relevant facts.

Appointing an independent evaluator is common when parents are giving conflicting versions on a serious matter. This evaluator will check out the different versions of events and report back to the court with what is considered to be an independent, unbiased evaluation.

Reports by an independent evaluator are always submitted to the court in writing and the evaluator can be cross-examined by either parent. The report will list those persons contacted, dates seen, summaries of interviews, and analysis of tests. The reports are detailed and make recommendations as to which parent should be awarded custody.

This report will also give specific visitation time periods for the non-custodial parent, and will outline ways to help the parents refine their child raising skills. Judges follow the custody recommendation from the evaluator 90% of the time. This high percentage should alert you to prepare yourself well if you will be undergoing an independent evaluation.

The independent evaluation report is a document that may be used in court and generally requires both parents to agree in writing beforehand. A judge will try to get the parents to sign the agreement before the evaluation is started because both parents think they will do well. After the report has been completed, and one parent is unhappy with the results, it will be very difficult for the other parent to override the recommendations made by an evaluator who has been agreed upon.

Selection of an evaluator is a critical and pivotal decision. Judges realize some evaluators have reputations as either father-biased or mother-biased. Judges try to find a fair method for selecting an evaluator and will often allow you the opportunity to interview several before a selection is determined.

**Note:** The judge provides parents a list of evaluators: One parent selects from the list, the other parent will then select one to actually do the evaluation.

When interviewing evaluators, keep in mind that the potential evaluator wants the business and is going to be very agreeable during the interview to get the job. Ask the evaluator for names of attorneys with whom they have worked with on other cases, and follow up.

Serious allegations made by one parent will trigger an evaluation report to be conducted by a mental health professional. This evaluation report can also be used as an investigative method of determining if children are in a dangerous environment. The urgency and speed with which an evaluation is conducted depend upon the length of time the case has been in the court system.

Listed here are some of the most common allegations that might require a report to be made by an evaluator:

- Abuse of alcohol or drugs.
- Physical violence.
- Neglect of the children.
- Sexual misconduct.
- Excessive school absences.
- Serious health risks.
- Mental instability.
- Substandard living conditions.
- No food in the refrigerator.
- All night partying.
- Immoral lifestyle.

There are many children living in dangerous situations and when this is the situation, agencies such as *Social Services* and *Child Protective Services, (C.P.S.)* get immediately involved. Both governmental agencies are authorized to intervene in situations where there is immediate danger to children, and they have the authority to remove the children from their home. In these cases where the children have been taken out of a dangerous environment, the case is handled in the Juvenile Court, and not in the Family Law Court. Ultimately, the children in the juvenile system can be put up for adoption.

The resources of these governmental agencies are limited. These agencies do not have the time, manpower nor the resources to conduct investigations that are generated by false and spiteful allegations.

**CASES IN THE SYSTEM:** When a case is already in the legal system and has false allegations, overblown charges, or misstatements, there is a paper trail that can be reviewed to determine authenticity. Judges want to know whether a child is in real danger or, if a parent is once again, "crying wolf." The number of child molestation and child endangerment charges increases dramatically when litigation over custody commences.

Judges and mediators are well aware that many parents make false charges to better their chances for winning custody. However, a parent's serious charges will still be investigated, and the standard precautionary measure is to order an evaluation by a neutral, third party professional. This evaluation can take months to complete and is an effective way to make the real truth known. When there is the possibility of child endangerment, judges would rather be "safe than sorry."

**CASES NOT IN THE SYSTEM:** Conversely, new cases involving serious allegations receive a rapid response by a judge because children new to the system have not been tracked and serious problems could exist. This is particularly true of children below school age, as these children are not protected by a safety net of school teachers. When a case is not yet in the legal system, an investigation of the allegations will be immediately looked into by a social worker. Such an emergency investigation is rapidly conducted, and the case will be heard in juvenile court, not family law court.

Court evaluations are lengthy and a considerable amount of time is spent in gathering up information, interviewing parents, children, and witnesses. Interactions between parent/child, home visits, psychological tests are all very time consuming. Further, the evaluator will spend many hours interpreting the information.

# PSYCHOLOGICAL TESTING

The written psychological testing given to the parents and children can be quite extensive. There are hundreds of tests and it is almost impossible to study up for every test that might be given. We have listed some more common psychological tests used. They have more tests than you have money, here are some of them:

- Ammons & Ammons Quick Test.
- Beck Depression Inventory.
- Bender Visual Motor Gestalt Test.
- Hooper Visual Organization Test.
- Minnesota Multiphasic Personality Inventory-2. (MMPI-2).
- Neuroticism Scale Questionnaire.
- Parenting Stress Index (PSI).
- Personality Inventory of Children (PSI).
- Sentence Completion Test.
- Shipley Institute of Living Scale.
- Symbol Digits Modalities Test.
- Wahler Test.

For more detailed information about a specific test, and the psychological parameters examined, consider going to a library, preferably university based, and ask the librarian for help. You can choose to consult with an independent psychologist to administer the tests you will be taking and then have the psychologist go over the test results with you. Informing yourself about psychological testing can be advantageous. It is well established that people involved in custody battles usually do not score well because they answer test questions in a way that makes them appear more favorable.

The cost of an evaluation can easily exceed $10,000. Evaluations consist of the following: Interviewing individuals with relevant information, interpretation of the test scores, clinical observations, and other facts provided to them. An evaluator will write a lengthy, detailed report and submit it to the judge with their recommendation as to which parent should have custody.

Evaluation reports often make other recommendations such as: visitation periods for non-custodial parent, parenting classes, monitoring, location restrictions, and counseling. Judges make the ultimate custody decision, and great consideration is given to the evaluator's written report.

## SHRINK CLASSIFICATIONS

It is important to understand the different classifications of mental health professionals as each classification has a specific area of expertise. The four you will most likely encounter are:

**Counselor - Mediator - Evaluator - Children's Therapist**

1.  **Counselor:** The generic term, *Counselor,* is used to describe almost any type of mental health professional. In custody matters it usually suggests a counselor who is providing individual therapy. When the treating counselor is asked to testify in court, judges are not inclined to listen to private conversations between the therapist and patient, as this relationship is considered privileged, similar to:

    - Attorney/Client.
    - Physician/Patient.
    - Priest/Confessor.
    - Clergyman/Penitent.

It is not a good tactic to bring your own counselor into court for favorable testimony. Judges realize you would not have this person testify unless they were going to speak highly of you. This one-sided counselor is called a **Unilateral Counselor,** a term that suggests partiality, someone on your payroll.

2.  **Mediator:** The generic term *Mediator,* is used to describe a mental health professional who works for the court. A court mediator works for the family law department and helps parents get through the legal process. Keep in mind, the mediator who is first assigned to your case will stay on your case as long as that mediator is an employee. The name used to describe the mediation office can vary in different courthouses, and may be termed:

    -   Mediation Office
    -   Family Court Services
    -   Conciliation Court

3.  **Evaluator:** This term, *Evaluator,* is used to describe an independent professional, someone in private practice, who primarily makes recommendations to the court. This professional is used by the judge to gather accurate and complete information.

    Costs for evaluations are usually split between the parents and can be very expensive. Just like a mediator, once an evaluator has been selected, this person will stay on your case for the duration. Therefore, be extremely careful not to antagonize or offend the individual who will have a very significant impact on your custody issue.

**4.**    **Children's Therapist:** The Children's Therapist is also a *Unilateral Counselor,* and this type of counselor treats the children, but does not evaluate them. There is a very big difference between a treating mental health professional, and an evaluating mental health professional. Each requires a different expertise.

If the child's therapist is called to testify in a court hearing, the confidences of the child may be violated and the trust established can be eroded. A child therapist does not want to testify on  confidential information about the children, as this could destroy the relationship.

When a child's therapist is subpoenaed to testify in court, a request to the judge is made for all private discussions to be excluded.  Information provided by the therapist can be enlightening,  however, the potential harm to children will outweigh the benefit of any such testimony. This potential damage to children means most judges prefer to hear from a child's therapist in chambers rather than in open court to preserve a child's trust in their therapist.

The various terms to describe the different types of mental health professionals can get confusing.  Judges are familiar with the different roles of each mental health professional and you will be much clearer in giving your presentation when you use the correct terminology. Try to be precise when referring to a specific mental health professional as qualifications and responsibilities of each type of counselor are somewhat different. You will make it easier follow the judge to follow the testimony if the roles of the counselors are correctly identified.

## "BEST INTEREST OF THE CHILDREN"

The universal guideline used by family law judges in making custody orders is:

*"Best Interest Of The Children."*

The magic words, *"Best Interest Of The Children"* is the standard phrase used by judges when making custody/visitation decisions. These five words describe the ultimate goal that judges, attorneys, mediators, and medical professionals try to achieve for every child. Strong disagreements arise between the experts when making determinations for a particular child. This standard is a subjective determination that will vary from case to case.

Custody battles consist of two imperfect people who also happen to be the parents. The real focus of custody litigation is not to determine which parent is "worser," rather who is best for the children. There is no family in America where one parent gets an "A" in child raising and the other parent gets an "F." All parents make mistakes, have problems, and strive to do better.

A judge is in the dilemma of making value judgments as to total strangers. The judge assesses parenting skills, measures the quality of each parent's household, determines which parent has the better of lifestyle, and other arbitrary decisions that affect the entire families' future. This judicial decision is not easy and requires him/her to weigh each parent's competency when making court orders. Because of this tremendous responsibility, judges rely upon input from competent sources who can offer helpful information about the children.

Family law judges make the decision, where the children will live at a time when a family is being blown apart. The judge relies on the mediator to help him/her decide which parent is better to raise the children. Judges want mediation to succeed. It is a well-established fact that parenting timeshare worked out in mediation results in more well-balanced children.

The custody issue can be fully resolved in mediation, and your participation is, therefore, critical. A miscommunication or little mistake can be catastrophic. Prepare for mediation as though your children's lives are at stake. They might be.

## OVERVIEW OF MEDIATION

The impact of your mediation session is according to the rules used by your local court system. The mediator assigned to your case will have an individual personality and style that has been refined over thousands of prior mediation sessions. Although mediators have different personalities and styles for conducting mediation, you do not need to worry about such variations as the strategies outlined here are successful no matter how the session is conducted.

Mediation involves only the parents at the first session. Attorneys, stepparents, grandparents, children and other family members and friends rarely participate in the mediation process. The mediator only talks with other third persons when the information obtained will be extraordinarily helpful. When there seems to be a lot of anger and hostility between the parents, the mediator will measure the "hostility" temperature, and then make the determination whether to see them separately or together.

**NO HOSTILITY:** When hostility is not a factor between the parents, the mediator conducts the session with both parents in the room attempting to resolve their differences with mutual "give and take."

**HOSTILITY:** When hostility level is high between the parents, the mediator will see each parent separately, may call in a second mediator, might want to see the children, and will verify each version of the facts.

Mediation sessions are conducted in a predictable fashion, so your participation can be well planned and rehearsed. Let's review the different ways in which a mediator can conduct the session:

- Discussions held jointly with both parents.

- Speak privately with each parent.

- Interview the children.

- Verify data with teachers, counselors, doctors, law enforcement officers or any other reliable persons.

- Consult with mental health professionals.

If parents reach a full agreement in the mediation session as to custody/visitation, then the terms and conditions are put into writing. Both parents must sign the agreement, then the judge signs, and this written agreement becomes an order of the court. This written agreement is called, a *"full stip."* (the legalese term for a full stipulation or a full agreement.)

It is a good tactical approach to make minor concessions during the mediation process if such efforts will bring you to a full agreement. This would avoid a court hearing, and spare you the high cost of litigation. The embarrassment of courtroom warfare is something no one should have to endure.

Before entering the mediation session, you must concede the following:

1. Counseling is a female-dominated profession. Expect to start the session as all fathers do as the "underdog."

2. If you are assigned to a male mediator, he will still be using traditional mom biased thinking that children belong with their mothers. Do not expect special consideration because the mediator is a male.

3. Don't antagonize, upset, or anger the mediator as he/she will be involved in your life for years to come.

4. Time in mediation is limited, so concentrate on resolving critical problems first.

5. Prepare, memorize, and rehearse a 10-minute presentation on your version of events.

6. You are going to know what "mud" mom will be slinging so rehearse anticipated responses to her "mudballs."

## CHAPTER 6

# CONDUCT IN MEDIATION

The mediator will have read court documents before your session and will be familiar with your case. You can expect the mediation session to commence as follows:

- Parents are given literature to read which explains the mediation process and articles on divorce and the effects on children.

- Parents are shown a video that gives instruction on ways to make the separation easier on the children.

- Parents receive a "pep-talk" on children's need for extra attention during this most difficult moment in a child's life. Cooperation between the parents is strongly urged.

The literature, video, and pep talk are used to get you and mom cooperating in your parenting approach with the children, even though the two of you loathe each other. Your reading of the pamphlets, and showing an active interest in the video, will be to your advantage. The mediator will notice your positive attitude and effort in the transition from parenting to co-parenting.

**Note:** A lack of interest in the parenting materials and video can reflect negatively on your parenting skill level. Act interested.

The parenting materials contain very helpful and valuable information. Pamphlets written by staff members about your local mediation office will give specific information on how mediation works with your local court system.

Mediation lasts about an hour and is generally limited to one session. Sometimes parents are requested to return with the children. Court documents are reviewed by the mediator, however other writings such as school, doctor, and police reports are not always reviewed due to time constraints. Keep writings you want the mediator to review limited to those specifically pertaining to the issue of custody/visitation. Child support and other financial matters are not discussed in mediation.

Answer questions with short answers and avoid a rambling narrative. A simple yes or no is often the best answer. Express confident body language by sitting up straight, leaning forward, maintaining eye contact, keeping your voice down, and using your hands for illustration. Refuse to engage in discussions about side issues that are irrelevant and time consuming.

# BASIC COURTESIES

There are basic human courtesies that set apart positive people with a good attitude from negative people with a bad attitude. These basic human courtesies should be used not only during your court hearing, but in everyday life. Demonstrating the ability to act in a civilized manner will portray you as an individual with the human skills needed to be a good parent.

We have provided you a list of common courtesies that should be used with the mediator. Look them over carefully and practice with friends those that do not come naturally to you. These basic human courtesies are very elementary, but if used, will help to win points with the mediator.

- Do be on time.
- Do have clean and neat appearance.
- Do show a confident attitude.
- Do dress conservatively.
- Do use eye contact.
- Do listen attentively.
- Do speak slowly.

*** 

- Do Not quarrel.
- Do Not show anger.
- Do Not overreact.
- Do Not interrupt.
- Do Not raise your voice.
- Do Not name-call.
- Do Not joke around.

## THE KEY IS TO BE LOW-KEY

The session begins with the mediator calling both parents into the office for an initial overview. You can effectively work with your mediator by keeping a positive, upbeat, and confident demeanor during the session. If mom is in fear of her safety, then the parents are kept in separate rooms, and your conduct must be very low-key. Do not show frustration, no matter how unfairly you think you are being treated. Avoid all confrontations with mom or the mediator. Arguing is ineffective, a waste of time, and reflects on your character.

If you think the mediation session is going to involve accusations of violence, be sure to keep your voice low, with no interruptions, and controlled body language. Using a loud voice, intense gestures, and stern facial expressions, will be interpreted as someone who is prone to violence. Keep your temper well in check. Your demeanor must be low-key and passive.

Allegations of violence are best countered by passive body language, controlled emotions, and a soft spoken voice. The absence of police reports or medical records should be pointed out to the mediator. The mediator will take a safe approach when allegations of violence are made. If this happens, you will find yourself in the position of being suspect until you can convince the mediator otherwise.

Mediators are incredibly patient people, therefore, it is sometimes hard to determine what problems they think are of utmost concern. Pay particular attention to the mediator's subtle changes in body movement or facial gestures, and maintain non-threatening eye contact.

## OBJECTIVES IN MEDIATION

Your objective in mediation is to convince the mediator that you are the better parent and it is best for the children to be with you. This goal is accomplished by delivering a precise, carefully rehearsed presentation, and not overreacting to adverse allegations. You will need to highlight your positive attributes, and mom's negative attributes without the session stooping to slinging "mudballs." Negative comments about mom must be expressed in a way that they cannot be misinterpreted as motivated by revenge. Such negative comments should be delivered in a concern for the effects on your children and not meanness to mom. Successful mediation requires effective preparation, good planning, and proper conduct. Any negative remarks about mom should begin with a qualifying statement, such as:

*"I really wish I didn't have to bring this up, but, our children are being exposed to . . ."*

Consider it a "given," that a mediator starts the session with the assumption the children belong with mom. You must not let the conversation quickly revolve around a proposed visitation schedule for you, but rather keep the conversation focused on a proposed visitation schedule for mom. The burden is on you to keep the dialogue centered on custody of the children to you, not visitation. Shift the dialogue away from difficult subject areas and into areas that you want to discuss by ignoring the question, and giving a rehearsed answer. Prepare short, punchy, sound-bytes for difficult subjects you anticipate being brought up.

**Note:** Take a tip from the politicians who don't directly answer a question, instead, give a rehearsed mini-speech.

Shift the conversation away from problem areas by calmly changing the subject to:

- Your superior parenting skills.
- The children's needs.
- Mom's deficiencies.

When discussing mom's deficiencies, do it in a way that will not embarrass or humiliate mom as your negative comments might be misinterpreted by the mediator. Don't let yourself get pulled down into a negative argument. Put positive spin on the negative issues by focusing on your main objective - custody. This is achieved by:

- Keeping discussions on key issues.
- Avoiding insignificant matters.
- Agreeing to minor compromises.

You now have an overview of mediation, and should begin preparing a detailed plan of action. Start your plan of action by writing a 10-minute presentation of your version of the events to present to the mediator. The 10-minute presentation should outline your position very succinctly. Also be ready to rebut those problem areas you know will be brought up by mom.

Generally speaking, females perform better in counseling type setting than males. This means most males are in an uphill climb during the mediation session. Remain calm even when you sense the mediator is siding with mom. Preparing and memorizing your 10-minute presentation will allow you to react positively to any adversities, and at the same time, not forget any of your main points.

## 10-MINUTE PRESENTATION

At the beginning of mediation, each parent will be asked to give their version of events. This can be a very critical moment because the parent going first will set the stage for the session. The 10-minute presentation should be memorized so delivery is given clearly and concisely. The presentation should accurately summarize specific family problems, and offer realistic solutions. Give your presentation with sincerity and conviction.

Memorizing the 10-minute presentation will lessen the likelihood of leaving out any key points. It will also alleviate some nervousness, and make you feel more confident. The most difficult part for most dads, when giving their speech to the mediator, is fending off interruptions by mom. Debating with mom when she interrupts, over trivial and irrelevant matters, will waste time and accomplish nothing. A dad needs to know he can respond later, in full detail, once the mediator indicates which of the interruptions needs clarification.

## BEGINNING THE DIALOGUE

Discussions in mediation fall into common patterns and have routine, standard, formula solutions used by the mediator. To help you through the mediation session, we have given examples of common scenarios that come up regularly between parents and mediators.

The following scenarios will help prepare you for what to expect in the mediation session, and give you insight on how to react in similar situations.

1. **Dad Starts - Mom Does Not Interrupt:**

Suppose dad begins the discussion with his interpretation of events and mom reacts with scared and defensive body language: Arms clasped tightly, a fearful look in her eyes, and other anxious reactions. In this situation a dad is likely to be perceived as controlling and abusive.

When a mediator sees this situation, the question comes up about whether mom's body language is indicative of a serious situation, or if she is being melodramatic to gain an advantage. Mom has set the mode, and now the mediator is going to key off dad in making a judgment.

If dad displays passive body language, speaks softly, and simply ignores mom's demeanor, then the mediator is likely to conclude that mom is overreacting. When faced with a fearful looking mom, it is critical that dad slow down and be mild mannered.

A dad jumping to initiate and dominate the discussion by, choosing the topic, speaking too loudly, over-talking, or displaying aggressive body language, will be viewed as a bully. Any aggressive dialogue will be counterproductive. Such behavior could be interpreted as manifestations of an angry person. A dad using this kind of behavior will lose any advantage made by going first, if conduct is perceived as anger rather than concern for his children. Therefore, be very careful to use controlled behavior and speak in a very soft voice if you are the first one asked to present version of events.

## 2.     Dad Starts - Mom Interrupts:

Suppose dad begins the discussion, and is then interrupted by a mom that over talks him. Dad now has only two choices:

### Stop Talking or Keep Talking

**Stop Talking:** Dad can stop talking and convey subtle body language to show his frustration. This indicates that the interrupting and over-talking mom is, "at it again." A mom interrupting will be interpreted as inconsiderate, rude and ill-mannered. Danger for dad is silence. If dad backs off and lets mom vent, this may result in dad not getting his version of events out to the mediator. Dad's strategy is not engage with mom, instead let the mediator admonish mom to let dad finish. At this point, dad should continue with his presentation exactly where he left off. Responding to mom's interruptions is ineffective, as dad then stops giving his prepared story and focuses on rebutting mom's charges.

**Keep Talking:** If dad keeps talking, completely ignoring mom's interruption, he must not raise his voice, and must keep eye contact with the mediator. A dad continuing to talk in a rational manner will force the mediator to take control of the session. The mediator will ask mom to please wait her turn and allow dad to finish. Dad's strategy is not to ask mom to please "be quiet," because it might be construed as attempting to be controlling. Also, it will leave dad open to quarreling and take time away from his presentation.

### 3. Mom Starts - Dad Interrupts:

Suppose mom starts the discussion with her version of events, and then dad interrupts to clarify or correct mom's story. The interruption of mom might be construed as rude and discourteous behavior. This is a bad tactical move for dad, as it gives the mediator the impression that dad is a controlling person. Dad's strategy is, to be polite and wait his turn despite charges alleged by mom. It is acceptable for dad to show his objections with subtle and appropriate facial grimaces and body language.

### 4. Mom Starts - Dad Does Not Interrupt:

Let's suppose that mom begins the discussion with her interpretation of events and dad listens politely, not interrupting, and appears well controlled. This is a good strategy for dad as his mannerisms and body language are those of a rational, responsible, and grounded personality. Rebutting each of mom's accusations only places further emphasis on her charges. Your best tactic in this situation, is to look the mediator in the eye and state, *"I disagree with everything she said."*

A good tactical move by dad is to wait his turn patiently, register disagreement, and take a long pause for effect. Then, when it is his turn to speak, continue with his 10-minute presentation. Dad must not respond to every allegation by mom. Responding to each of moms' charges, means the conversation will focus on those charges. This will waste time and end up in a "tit for tat," squabble.

Impressions made with the mediator will pigeonhole you. When in front of the mediator, project adult behavior, be well mannered and act like a responsible individual. Be sure to show admiration for the mediator by letting him/her know you respect the difficulty of their high-pressure job of dealing with the constant stress of family breakups. This should be expressed with much sincerity and not as attempts to "brown-nose" the mediator.

## DOCUMENTS PRESENTED IN MEDIATION

Take written documents that will help to confirm your account of important events. Your having the documents readily at hand enhances credibility even though the mediator may not read the paperwork. Important documents include:

- Diaries.
- Calendars.
- School records.
- Doctor letters.
- Police reports.
- Psychological evaluations.
- Official writings.

Take all writings that support your version of events into the mediation session. However, realize each mediator responds differently when given written documents by parents. Each individual mediator has his/her own policy about reading written documents. Some mediators do not want to see written documents under the rationale that mediation will turn into a "paper war." Other mediators will scan through the written documents asking for clarification on their major concerns.

## FIGHTING FIRE WITH FIRE

Females are much more skilled than males when it comes to verbal communication. Males are raised to be strong and silent, and not complain when things don't go their way. Males are expected to "take it like a man." Conversely, females are not criticized for displaying emotions.

Histrionics is the word used by counselors to describe exaggerated body movements, something you would expect from an actress. Females use histrionics as a form of communication and such conduct is tolerated. Males using histrionics are a cause for alarm. This male and female double standard is a fact you must accept. It occurs in the work place, home, mediation and court. You are not going to change this double standard.

If your mediation session develops into a laundry list of complaints from mom, don't fall into the trap of responding likewise. The session will turn into a spitting contest and males always lose when arguing with a female. If you find yourself up against verbal insults, do not "fight fire with fire." The appropriate response is to appear aloof and above the fray.

There should be no big surprises in the mediation session as you know the complaint list. Discussion will be predictable; therefore, you can plan and rehearse your participation. Prioritize the issues and stick with major problem areas. Defer discussing minor concerns until the important issues are resolved. A positive attitude and mature manner is reflected when you concentrate on major problems and do not drift off into trivial subjects. Appear confident, and in control even when adversarial comments are being made about your behavior.

## TERMINOLOGY AND PHRASEOLOGY

In mediation, you must use the right terminology and phraseology so you do not come across as a revengeful dad. Knowing specific terminology and phraseology to use or not use in mediation, will help you gain an advantage with the mediator.

We will be giving you a couple of important examples of specific terminology and phraseology to learn, practice and then memorize. The specific language and words should be a part of your vocabulary when in mediation.

**1.    Terminology all fathers should use in mediation when registering complaints against mom:**

The first rule for all fathers going through mediation is to NEVER start off a sentence in the following way:

*"Ann is a . . ."*

*"She did . . ."*

*"This woman does not . . ."*

If you begin a sentence with *"mom's name," "she/her," "this woman,"* or similar pronoun, it sounds as though you are criticizing, blaming, and accusing. The mediator may view you as having an overbearing personality, or see you as a person who is shifting all the blame for the family problems on mom. You do not want to be perceived as a name-calling, mom-blaming father, who refuses to accept his own responsibility and is in a state of denial.

This ploy will end up boomeranging on you, and it will cause sympathy toward mom. You can express a complaint about mom but in a way that doesn't offend her or make you look bad. You can do this by rewording the phrase beginning with the word *"I."* For instance, let's suppose your complaint is that mom keeps a filthy house and you need to tell the mediator about the dirty dishes, unsanitary bathrooms, unclean clothes, etc. This is a valid complaint that needs to be told.

Here is an example of a correct and incorrect way to deliver a message to the mediator when a complaint needs to be brought up in mediation.

**Incorrect:** If you start the complaint by saying, *"Ann's house is a pigpen,"* you have made a charge that will force the mediator to decide the accuracy of your complaint. Then, the mediator will decide about whether you are over stating the situation.

**Correct:** The way to express the above complaint and not appear blaming , is to say, *"I am very concerned about the living conditions of our children."*

We have just given you an example of the correct way to present the problem of moms keeping a dirty house. You can use this same technique when you want to present other problems that need to be brought to the attention of the mediator such as: Drug use, excessive drinking, poor parenting, immoral activities, other serious problems.

The use of the word *"I"* to start a sentence denotes your concern and does not come across as an attempt to blame. Each complaint you have can be reworded so you begin each sentence with the word *"I."* Practice talking about your complaints by starting with the word *"I."* This is not a male's normal way of speaking, so it will take practice for you to talk this way using the proper technique.

Here are a couple of examples you should memorize so that concern for the children is what the mediator hears:

*"I am concerned . . ."*

*"I worry that . . . "*

*"I am afraid that . . ."*

Whenever you begin the phrase with the word *"I,"* it will denote an inward concern on your part, and will not be viewed as an accusatory type of statement. Now what you have done is, put the problem in front of the mediator in a non-accusatory manner. This will force the mediator to deal with the seriousness of the problem to protect your children.

After starting the complaint off with the word *"I,"* refer to how the problems affect *"our"* children.

*Always, Say "OUR" Children, Not "MY" Children*

Begin each complaint with the word *"I"* and then focus the conversation about how the problem is adversely affecting *"our"* children.

Always use the term:

### *"OUR" Children, not "MY" Children*

Your problems must be registered with the mediator in a neutral way. You will need to begin a sentence with the word *"I."* Then, focus the discussion on how the specific problem is affecting *"our"* children.

The proper way to communicate your problem areas in mediation is to express your complaints in the following manner.

> *"I am concerned about the use of drugs in front of "our" children as it is a bad example for them. "Our" children may accidentally put the drugs in their mouths."*

> *"I worry that mom's new boyfriend is using corporal punishment and that "our" children are being physically abused."*

> *"I am afraid for the safety of "our" children as they are always left with immature babysitters, neighbors, or other strangers."*

Again, the way you do this is to start a phrase with the word *"I"* to identify the problem, and then focus on the affect the problem has on *"our"* children.

The communication technique you have just learned, is something you must rehearse repeatedly as males do not normally speak in this manner. The biggest challenge for a male during the mediation session is to convey information to the mediator in a non-judgmental way. Practice this technique over and over again until it feels right.

**2. Terminology to be used by fathers when responding to complaints made about him by mom in mediation:**

Do not respond to each complaint made by mom, as responding to every accusation will only waste time and place you in the position of constantly defending yourself. Keep all your discussions with the mediator centered on your concerns for the children. Then, let the mediator decide which complaints of mom's need clarification. If in doubt, ask the mediator which problems you need to address.

After the mediator has identified a problem area and asks for your version, make sure you start your response off with the word *"I."* Then, continue the discussion focusing on how the problem is affecting *"our"* children. Always respond to mom's complaints by using the same technique, using the words, *"I"* and *"our,"* at the beginning of a sentence and then proceed to give your version of events. Once again, we will be giving you an incorrect and correct way to communicate with the mediator.

This technique may not seem significant to you now, but when you get into mediation, and respond as we have suggested using the words, *"I"* and *"our,"* you will see from the reaction of the mediator how well this tactic works.

Here is another example of an incorrect and correct way to respond to the mediator when mom says you have a drinking problem:

**Incorrect:** Do not respond by saying, "s*he's accusing me of alcoholic abuse because her father is abusing alcohol and, therefore, "she" sees an alcoholic behind every tree.*"

**Correct:** Always start with the word *"I"* and say; *"I do have a drink occasionally, but I have never had a drunk driving charge nor have I ever missed a day of work due to a hangover. Our children have never been affected by my having an occasional drink. I am willing to stop all drinking if I need to prove that I do not have a drinking problem.*"

or

**Correct:** *"I am a recovering alcoholic (the A.A. term), and I have not had a drink in two years and I consider myself a better parent because I understand the serious consequences caused by drinking. Thus, I feel I am a better role model for our children.*"

You know in advance the complaints mom is going to be making about your behavior. Practice rebutting these complaints by using the words *"I"* and *"our"* in front of a mirror or in your car driving to and from work. Practice this same rehearsal whether you are presenting mom's problems or whether you are rebutting mom's accusations.

Sometimes, both the parents are really decent people and there are no complaints from either side. If this is your situation, you should still use the same communication technique as above, using the words *"I"* and *"our."* Center the conversation on why you are able to provide a healthier, and more stable environment for raising *"our"* children.

The proper way to communicate your desires is in the following manner:

**Correct:** *"I" have always prepared the children's meals, given them baths, read them bedtime stories, taken them to doctor appointments. I have also attended their school conferences and have participated in their extracurricular activities. Our children would be seriously affected if I were not able to stay involved in the day-to-day lives of "our" children."*

## COMPROMISING IN MEDIATION

Compromise is expected by both parties when in the mediation session. A parent not willing to compromise will be perceived as uncooperative. You must show flexibility and a reasonable attitude by compromising on minor issues. You do not want those issues that you are firm on to be construed as stubborn positions that indicate you are an uncooperative parent.

A parenting plan that is agreeable to both parents takes not only compromise, but also commitment. Parenting plans mutually worked out in mediation have a much greater success rate and result in happier, more well-adjusted children.

A mediator experiences situations all the time where a full agreement on custody breaks down over a minor ego-point by one parent. When there is no cooperation between the two parents, agreements unravel, and the case must go to a court hearing. The parent seen in court as the obstinate one by the judge, can end up getting less than was originally conceded to in mediation.

When a court hearing is required, the judge wants to know why the parents could not come to a full agreement in mediation. Fathers need to let the judge know they tried very hard to come to an agreement in mediation, and made every effort to settle the family problems so as to not waste the court's time.

## THE NIGHT BEFORE MEDIATION

1. Formulate a parenting plan on paper and take it with you to mediation. Your parenting plan should outline the most important needs of your children.

2. Focus your thoughts on your parenting role and separate out your feelings about mom. Temporarily bury any anger and hurt that you have towards mom.

3. Identify those areas of need that are particularly applicable to your own children, and decide how these needs can be met with continuity and stability.

4. Acknowledge that your children need a good relationship with both parents and resolve not to speak badly about mom in their presence. Children will always love both their parents no matter what is said about them.

5. Recognize your children's care should be shared equally between both of you. Fathers have rights over relatives, babysitter, neighbor, or boyfriend.

6. Devise a parenting plan that considers your children's needs over those of your own: Children's schooling, activities, and emotional needs.

7. Resolve to keep all communications open concerning the children. Communicating with mom through attorneys is very expensive.

8. Concentrate your mediation preparation on the present needs of the children rather than on your problems with mom.

9. Keep the children's best interest uppermost in your mind and allocate your time on WHAT is wrong, rather than on WHO is wrong.

10. The night before mediation, lay out clean, pressed clothes, gas your car, organize your paperwork, have money for parking, and get a good night sleep. You want to make a great impact in the morning.

# CHAPTER 7

# ACTION IN THE COURTROOM

When a full parenting agreement is not reached during the mediation process as to custody/visitation, then the decision is left up to the judge. There are no juries in family law. The mediation session helps the court in identifying the issues that are the most important problem areas in your case. The mediator knows the thought process of individual judges, therefore, what you perceive as your most important issues may not be deemed likewise by the mediator. Consider mediation as a preview for what will likely be of greatest interest to the judge.

Do not be too concerned if you were unable to reach a mutual agreement as to custody/visitation of your children during mediation. You will have your day in court and a judge will make the ultimate decision.

## MEDIATION/COURT HEARING TIMELINE

Court hearings start on the same day as mediation in some court houses, and weeks later in others. Learning the time frame of mediation session/court hearing sequence is very important to know. If mediation is held on the same day as the court hearing, preparation must be done well in advance. If your court hearing is held at a later date, then you will have more time to prepare.

You may have to do both mediation and the court hearing on the same day. If this is the situation, you will have no time to prepare. Therefore, it is imperative you have all your necessary paperwork ready before your mediation session.

or

When court is at a later date, you will have the extra time to regroup, address new problems, and gather up any additional information required for your court hearing.

On your fieldtrip to the courthouse, ask at the mediation office about the court hearing timeline after mediation. Knowing approximately when your court date is will be helpful in planning your strategy, and give you time to organize any data needed for court. Sometimes information and statements made in mediation are taken out of context. Use the extra time to gather evidence which can be used to rebut incorrect information or statements.

# THE COURTROOM

Each morning a judge looks out over the bench at a group of new faces, with the identical problems as the previous day. divorcing parents have similar, underlying emotional forces that are at work. Judges are well aware of the passions that fuel the litigants. On your fieldtrip, visit the family law courtrooms, and watch the dramas unfold. Observing cases in action will give you a perspective on the proper courtroom demeanor and procedures. You will also see the interaction between judges, court personnel, attorneys, and litigants.

Let's use the football analogy:

**FOOTBALL GAMES:** The teams, referees, fans and stadiums change from Sunday to Sunday, however, the game remains the same.

**COURT HEARINGS:** The judges, parents, children, and attorneys change from day to day, but the human drama remains the same.

You learned the game of football and you can learn the game of a court hearing. You don't need to know every picky little rule to play football, similarly, you don't need to know every picky little court rule for a court hearing. Learning the procedural rules for court hearings is simplified by the fact that you only have to learn and understand about one specific type of court hearing:

## *A  CUSTODY  HEARING*

# PIGEONHOLE

It is common for a family law judge to conduct over fifty hearings a week. Judges with these large caseloads, see repeating issues that come up on a daily basis and have developed their own individual policies to solve these similar family problems. The recurring courtroom scenarios are then mentally categorized by a judge and put into a . . . *pigeonhole.*

The danger of pigeonholing is a judge can misconstrue information, and place you in the wrong pigeonhole, resulting in the wrong judicial remedy. Therefore, once a case is incorrectly pigeonholed, it is likely to stay there for a very long time. It is vitally important that the judge correctly interpret your situation.

A major goal on your fieldtrip is to find out each judge's policy regarding repeating problems. The only way to do this is, to sit in on several family law cases. Judges identify problems by listening to facts presented, mentally placing them into specific pigeonholes, and then make standard orders designed for the specific pigeonhole. Try and find out from your mediator how individual judges respond to certain issues.

Family law judges make decisions on the issue of custody by listening to many, many, parents, experts, and witnesses. They get fooled less and less as time goes on. After hearing thousands of custody cases, a judge develops a "sixth sense," and can spot the right tree in the forest. This perceptive ability is wonderful when it works, but is devastating when it doesn't. If a judge perceives false allegations for what they are, great. If not, false allegations can take years to straighten out.

Keep Out Of The Wrong Pigeonhole!!!

## EFFECTIVE PARTICIPATION

A court hearing can be a very confusing experience for the average person. Do not overly concern yourself with the many technicalities of the court proceedings as the judge will keep things fair to both sides. You should, however, learn the overview and flow of a court hearing to properly understand what is going on, what is expected of you, and when you are needed to participate. Knowledge of the procedural maze will give you the peace of mind and confidence needed to focus your energies on the presentation of your case. Your participation in court will be much more effective if you concentrate on "strategizing," rather than on the procedural nuances. Stay mentally ahead of events so you can think hard about alternative ways of dealing with your judge.

Don't lose sight of your purpose in court as the procedural aspects of a court hearing can take centerstage and overpower the custody issue. Your objective in court is to give correct factual information at the appropriate time. Knowing what information to give, and when to give it, is a conscious choice that you will have to make. There are a couple of explosive areas that you definitely want to avoid:

1.  **INTERRUPTING:** Judges hear court cases in a specified order, and they do not like it when litigants interrupt the flow of the hearing. Judges get very upset when a litigant talks out of turn or interrupts court proceedings. Litigants that are unfamiliar with the court proceedings are more inclined to interrupt, over-talk, or speak out of turn. These litigants do not realize that they will have an opportunity to tell their full story.

2.   **RAMBLING:**   Litigants have limited time in court to give their version of the story because of the many other litigants waiting their turn. Judges are considerate of these waiting litigants and get annoyed when litigants ramble on about issues that are not relevant to their case. Judges want to hear stories from litigants that are:

**clear - concise - relevant - on point**

Rambling on about irrelevant issues only causes discord, wastes the court's time, and irritates the judge. If the judge wants a litigant to move on to another issue because a point has been made, then do it. A litigant's participation level and demeanor will be carefully weighed by a judge.

The common thread for a father who has won custody of his children is persistence. Fathers who have won custody all started with the same uphill struggle. The winning equation in a court custody battle is:

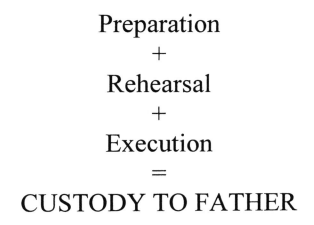

Preparation

+

Rehearsal

+

Execution

=

CUSTODY TO FATHER

## CHAPTER 8

# COURT HEARINGS EXPLAINED

In family law cases, court hearings are separated into three types of hearings and must fit within the parameters of the three hearings.

|  |  |  |
|---|---|---|
| *Pre-Trial* | | *Post-Trial* |
| *Hearings* | *TRIAL* | *Hearings* |

Family law judges can conduct all three different types of court hearings within a given day, and then follow different judicial guidelines for each. However, the guiding standard for all judicial decisions about children, no matter which type of hearing will be what is:

*"In The Best Interest Of The Children"*

Judges handle custody orders differently and depending on which phase of a court hearing a litigant is in.

- Where a litigant is situated in the court proceeding.

- Where the case is positioned in the phase of the litigation.

When a court hearing is set for either pre-trial or post-trial, then this hearing is referred to as, *"Order to Show Cause"* and are more commonly called an *"O.S.C."* The Order To Show Cause is set for a pre-trial or post-trial court hearing when a parent is asking for either initial custody orders or is requesting some change in the existing order. The parent responding to the request can then appear at the O.S.C. court hearing to give legitimate reasons, (show cause), about why the orders requested should not be granted. You need to know if your court hearing is pre-trial, trial, or post-trial.

1. **Pre-Trial Hearing:** A pre-trial hearing is a court hearing that is held before trial, and orders given at this time are called, *Temporary Orders.*

2. **Trial:** Trial is generally four to six months after starting litigation and orders made at the time of trial are expected to be far more permanent. Court orders made at time of trial are called, *Judgments.*

3. **Post-Trial Hearing:** A post-trial hearing is held after the trial and is necessary because of changes in the children's circumstances. If any new court orders are issued at this time, they are called, *Post-Judgment Orders.*

A judge's initial inquiry when he/she receives your case file, is to find out if the hearing is for pre-judgment orders. Learn the different rules of procedure followed by the judge in each of the three different types of court hearings. Knowing the three types of hearings will help to keep your testimony within the procedural parameters and not waste time. An overview of the three types of hearings is next.

## PRE-TRIALS

Pre-trial hearings start with your first court appearance and are those scheduled hearings which are held before the actual trial. The initial pre-trial hearing is held because parents have failed to reach a full agreement regarding custody in the mediation session.

This first court hearing is very critical because it sets the placement and rhythm of the case. Subsequent judicial decisions are made after looking at the initial placement. Custody decisions made at a pre-trial court hearing are temporary orders and you will hear the legal term, *pendente lite,* being used by attorneys. This pendente lite order determines initial living arrangements for the children and the judge is charged with, *preserving the status quo.* The residence of the children is the status quo and a critical factor at this hearing and judges are conscious of the shifting custody that goes on prior to the first court hearing.

Temporary orders include: Child support, spousal support, exclusive use or possession of automobiles, and some distribution of each parent's personal belongings. When a pre-trial hearing is held at the time of parent's separation, property issues are not as important as custody issues and often left until time of trial. This initial hearing is meant to stabilize children's lives, making as few changes as necessary, resulting in the least disruption for children.

# Pendente Lite Orders

Pre-judgment orders are temporary orders made by a judge at a pre-trial hearing and termed, *pendente lite,* a Latin phrase meaning, "pending the litigation." The main thrust of pendente lite orders is to preserve the status quo of children. This initial order is crucial in a custody battle as it locks custody into place. Judges at pre-trial hearings know that by the time parents get on to the trial, both children and parents will have adjusted to the temporary orders. A pre-trial hearing is the most important hearing because at trial the judge looks at the temporary orders when making the permanent custody orders.

## Preserve The Status Quo

Pre-trial orders are only temporary and intended to keep the children stabilized during the court proceedings and this effort is to *preserve the status quo.* The judge at the first pre-trial hearing wants to keep the children intact with few changes in their lives. Judges are aware that when parents separate, the family is going to be experiencing major adjustments. Maintaining a normal and stable environment for the children is what the judge wants to accomplish at the pre-trial hearing.

Children from a broken home experience deep emotional distress. Judges at this early stage of the case will make orders that are least disruptive for the children: Keeping them sleeping in their own beds, residing in the same home, going to the same schools, playing with the same friends, and receiving support from familiar teachers. Judges know children cope better during family breakups if the other areas of their lives remain stable. There is enough disruption without a new neighborhood, school, friends, teachers, activities, and other changes brought on by the family breakup.

### The Right Pigeonhole

Judges at pre-trial hearings make decisions on those issues needing immediate attention and the orders are "only temporary." However this hearing pigeonholes your case and will always be used as a "benchmark" for subsequent orders. Therefore, just prior to a first court hearing there is gamesmanship and groundshifting.

It is not uncommon for a parent to take possession of their children, exclude the other parent, and then hustle into court asking that the status quo be preserved. Judges are aware of this groundshifting tactic, and will take steps necessary to unwind any unfair maneuvers. A father involved in ligitimate groundshifting must be prepared to answer the charge of a strong-arm technique.

### MULTIPLE PRE-TRIALS

Court time is scarce and in high demand. Citizens want disputes resolved in a timely fashion. Judges do not want the court system overburdened by litigants requesting multiple hearings. Judges do not mind fine-tuning previous court orders, but loathe revisiting problems that have been adequately assessed at previous court hearings. Judges do not tolerate litigants coming to court in the hopes that he/she will eventually have his/her way.

Significant changes in circumstances do warrant another hearing, but minor glitches will be resolved at time of trial. A repetitive request from an unhappy camper only irritates a judge. Appearing as if "judge shopping" or wanting a "second bite at the apple" will be disastrous.

*Pendente lite* court hearings attempt to *preserve the status quo,* and should not be used as a "second bite of the apple." Be careful not to get in the wrong *pigeonhole.*

# SETTLEMENT CONFERENCES BEFORE TRIAL

The purpose of a settlement conference is to narrow the issues and, hopefully avoid the necessity of a trial. The settlement conference will give parents a realistic picture of what can happen in court if a trial becomes necessary.

Settlement conferences are effective because they force parents, attorneys, and the judge to intently focus on the problems. To avoid a costly and time-consuming trial, judges encourage settlements as trials are emotionally draining, very expensive, and produce strange results. Concessions made by parents in the settlement conference result in agreements that are longer lasting. Each and every courthouse has its own procedures for settlement conferences:

- *Mandatory Settlement Conferences - (M.S.C.)* Require the attendance of both parties.

- *Voluntary Settlement Conferences - (V.S.C.)* Helpful when the differences are narrow.

A settlement conference is held at the courthouse with the assistance of a judge and is conducted according to local rules:

- Some courts only set conferences for long-cause matters, others have conferences before every trial.

- Some courts have assigned trial judges to conduct the conferences, others prefer a separate judge.

- Some judges will only speak to attorneys, others will talk with both parents and the attorney.

# THE TRIAL

The essential elements in any trial are for a knowledgeable and fair judge to determine controversies. The facts presented are set in place and the legal issues are decided in court. Trials are overwhelming to litigants, so we have devised a simple formula to help you understand this complicated procedure.

## Legal vs.Tactical

**Legal:**

Laws/codes.
Local rules.
Policies of individual judges.

**Tactical:**

Effective organization of facts.
Selection and order of witnesses.
Presentation of evidence.

Family law trials are unique in that there are no juries. In divorce trials, now called dissolution of marriage, there are issues other than custody/visitation problems that need to be addressed. Property division, debt allocation, retirement benefits, tracing problems, payment credits, and other financial issues are dealt with at time of trial as each party has had enough time to do discovery. The custody issue tends to be short-changed at trial as attention is focused on property and debt issues.

Trials involving custody issues require participation of mental health professionals, teachers, family members, minister, neighbors, and law enforcement officers. Temporary orders have not resolved the custody issues and parents are ready for warfare.

# PATERNITY TRIALS

Custody of children born to unwed parents also referred to as paternity, cannot be accomplished in a dissolution action. For a judge to have authority to make custody orders in a paternity case, a court filing termed a Paternity Lawsuit must be filed.

**Note:** A paternity action does not include property issues, even when the parents purchased items together, and property issues must be resolved in civil or small claims courts.

The participants in a paternity action are funneled through family law court system just like divorcing couples. The main issue in a paternity case is whether the alleged father is the biological father. A bitter, spiteful mom will claim the alleged father is not the biological father making things so expensive and difficult, the alleged father quits the contest. Judges are convinced that D.N.A. testing is without error and will give accurate scientific evidence about whether the alleged father is the real father.

Paternity testing is performed by the analysis of D.N.A. in the blood. D.N.A. testing is very sophisticated and has reached a level where it is possible for persons to be tested without a third party. Thus, D.N.A. is only needed from the father and child, not mom. Paternity testing results range from 0% to 99.9%, however actual results only come back at 0% or in the high 90%. Judges rely on D.N.A. testing at trial to determine paternity. The classic defense of a revengeful mom is to delay testing, establish status quo, and block father out of the child's life until trial.

# PROCEDURE OF A TRIAL

At time of trial the judge will look back at the temporary orders as a guide in making permanent orders. Trial judges have the advantage of hindsight and over-rely on previous orders. Family law trials involving custody of the children, are only needed when parents have not agreed on who will have primary custody after a lengthy period of time in the legal system. A custody trial is emotionally draining, time consuming, and very expensive.

The order of a trial is determined by who filed first. The person filing the action will present evidence first at a trial.

*Plaintiff* in a civil lawsuit.
*Petitioner* in family law.

The other party is termed:

*Defendant* in a civil lawsuit.
*Respondent* in family law.

Before beginning a family law trial, some judges will take both attorneys into his/her office, chambers, for a conference to familiarize the judge with the facts and problems of the case.

**Note:** Chambers conferences in custody cases should be avoided, as the fastest talker can mislead and intentionally place the case in the wrong pigeonhole.

Both sides make an opening statement for the purpose of identifying issues, outlining evidence, and requesting orders. After each side has given an opening statement, the petitioner begins presenting evidence through witnesses.

# TRIAL BRIEF

You and your attorney will draft up a written statement entitled, *Trial Brief* for presentation to the trial judge at time of trial. The trial brief document is intended to familiarize the judge with the remaining problems of your case and inform him/her of the position of each parent regarding those particular problems. It will outline your position, and aid the judge in understanding the complexities of your case and the orders you are requesting.

A trial brief on custody issues will include the following:

Present custodial arrangements.

Current problems.

Recommended solutions.

The trial brief can include documents, declarations, charts, graphs, school/doctor records, photos, or any other information that will help the judge to make an enlightened decision. Careful consideration should be given to the preparation of a trial brief as it is the first impression received by the trial judge.

Problems that have occurred after the initial, temporary orders, must be described in specific detail in the trial brief. The trial judge reads the trial brief before observing the parents. Judges begin formulating opinions from the facts presented in the trial brief and mentally maneuver the case toward a specific pigeonhole. Therefore, it is very important for the trial brief to project your true character. The objective in a father trial brief is to include anything and everything that can influence the case in his favor.

## POST TRIALS

Post-judgment hearings are held after a trial has been conducted. Family law courts retain jurisdiction over children until they reach the age of majority. A request for a post-judgment hearing can only be made when there are significant change of circumstances as judges do not have the time to listen to the same story rehashed repeatedly. The judge only wants to hear about new circumstances regarding the children that may require a change in the present orders. A judge will make new orders to fit changing situations, but will be upset if it appears that the reason a parent is back in court (making the same request) is in the hopes that another judge will view the same situation in a different light.

### Change Of Circumstances

A significant *change of circumstances* in the children's lives is required before a judge will modify prior judicial orders with respect to the issue of custody/visitation. When a parent requests a change in the prior judicial orders, the requesting parent needs to show the court new or significant changes affecting the children. A parent with a pattern of making constant requests, might be considered a disgruntled litigant by a judge. If you have a legitimate reason for coming back to court, it is best for you to consolidate all the problems and make just "one big issue" the reason for requesting a new hearing. The big issue opens the door to judicial consideration and gives the opportunity to fix minor problems that might not otherwise warrant a court hearing.

Note: Custody orders are not "etched in stone." A court has jurisdiction over children until age eighteen (18). Any modifications to present court orders can be changed until children reach such age.

Valid and invalid circumstances calling for change custody orders are as follows:

## Invalid:
- Attempts at judge shopping.
- Made by a vexatious litigant.
- Motivated by revenge.
- Reconsideration in disguise.

## Valid:
- Mom wants to move the children's residence, often out of state.

- Mom sabotages dads contact with the children.

- Moms neglectful parenting of the children.

- Moms alcohol or drug abuse.

- Moms boyfriend is a danger to the children.

- Children are exposed to dirty and unsanitary living conditions.

- Children want to make changes in their present living arrangements.

- Children are doing poorly in school.

- Children are disciplinary problems.

- Children aren't getting proper medical/dental care.

# EX-PARTE HEARINGS

Court hearings can be conducted on very short notice in emergency situations when there is no time to wait for an open court date. This emergency proceeding which is held with little or no notice is called, an ex-parte hearing. The Latin term, *ex-parte*, means one side only. Notice required for an ex-parte hearing is decided by the local procedure, set by each individual court and can vary from:

- Four (4) hours notice.
- Twenty-four (24) hours notice.
- Specific days only.
- Reservations needed.

Relief requested at an ex-parte hearing must be based on an emergency and show irreparable injury to the party initiating the ex-parte hearing. Irreparable injury is defined as, a harm that cannot be solved by money. There can be a significant tactical advantage in requesting ex-parte orders, as these ex-parte orders can re-position a case.

**Example:** An ex-parte "kick-out" order of the father, based on domestic violence, will establish custody with the mother.

Ex-parte orders are temporary and only last until an Order to Show Cause hearing, (O.S.C), which is conducted within a few weeks of the ex-parte hearing. The O.S.C. hearing is necessary in order to allow the other party time to adequately respond to allegations made at the ex-parte hearing.

# ORDER OF BATTLE

The order of battle for a court hearing has been designed to give both sides of the controversy an equal opportunity in court to present their version of the story. Evidence is given by each side of the controversy and have an equal opportunity to:

- Present evidence through uninterrupted testimony.

- The right to cross-examine testimony.

- Bring in witnesses to speak on their behalf.

The order of battle in a court hearing has been developed over many centuries and is not perfect. However, the American legal system is considered the fairest in existence. Trust in the judicial system and rely on the wisdom of the judge.

Testimony given is kept in a strict order and sequence and can be very confusing to a litigant. Understand that you will be given a full opportunity to give your version of events to the judge, however the order in which evidence is presented has a tremendous tactical advantage.

Understanding the sequence and manner in which evidence is presented in a court hearing, will enable you to keep up with the fast pace and stay mentally ahead of your opposition. This will free up your thought process to concentrate on upcoming problems so you can make adjustments necessary during the court proceeding. Watch television, go to the movies, and rent videos pertaining to courtroom dramas, and study the strategies and tactics used in these dramas.

## CASE-IN-CHIEF

The person requesting the court hearing is called, the *moving party*, and the other person is called, the *responding party*. The moving party gets to go first in presenting evidence. This evidence presentation is called, *case-in-chief*. After the moving party has concluded giving evidence, the moving party "rests" and the responding party presents their case-in-chief. Each side gets an equal opportunity to tell their story. Confusion arises because each witness that testifies will be cross-examined during their case-in-chief.

Cross-examination of each witness is conducted to test the honesty of witnesses. It is inappropriate to try to give your version of events at the time mom is on the witness stand giving her testimony. This is when you should just sit back, try to relax, take notes, respectfully observe, and act your age. Use mature conduct by not interrupting, overreacting, or badgering your attorney. Any immature conduct on your part will reflect adversely upon you. You will have the opportunity to give your version of events at the time of your case-in-chief.

The case-in-chief period of the hearing is difficult to understand for litigants. To clear up some confusion, we have created four groupings to simplify and clarify:

- Who goes first.

- If you are called as a witness.

- Purpose of cross-examination.

- How to conduct yourself at the council table.

1. **The person requesting the court hearing goes first except at trial when person initially filing goes first.**

At a pre-trial or post-trial hearing, the parent requesting the court hearing presents evidence first. This can be advantageous, since the judge hears this version first and temporarily locks in the facts. The side going second has the burden of both, disproving the previous version, and offering a second version of events. The side going first will want to present inflammatory, derogatory, and highly prejudicial facts as a way to set the stage.

At trial, the parent originally filing the action will present evidence first, however, the trial judge will have reviewed the file, and the advantage of going first does not have as great an advantage.

2. **Being called as a witness during mom's case-in-chief.**

If you are called as a witness during moms case-in-chief, confusion arises because you are being called upon to aid mom's case, not to tell your story. Therefore, being called during mom's case-in-chief means you will be treated as an adverse witness. This time won't be counted against your allotted court time.

**Caution:** You can only respond to questions asked by mom's attorney. You will not be allowed to give a full explanation until the time of your own case-in-chief. Listen carefully before answering questions and keep answers brief. Use yes or no answers whenever possible.

3.      **Purpose of cross-examination - mom's case-in-chief.**

Cross-examination is used to clarify or disprove testimony of mom or her witnesses, and challenging their version of events. Cross-examination is limited to the areas covered during direct testimony. Witnesses' are tested for bias, credibility, believability, and overall truthfulness. Honest witnesses give statements that are accurate, yet they leave an impression which is totally false. Cross-examination of witnesses is designed to feret out inaccuracies, disclose half-truths, and identify selective memory.

4.      **Conduct at the council table - mom's case-in-chief.**

The following are some tips to remember when you are at the council table listening to mom testify.

-       Avoid interrupting during mom's case-in-chief as such behavior will come across as immature. Sit quietly and calmly during any testimony mom gives that is either false or misleading. You will have the opportunity during your case-in-chief to tell your version of events, rebut allegations made by mom, and set the record straight.

-       Avoid overreacting during any adverse testimony, because judges watch for reactions. Responding in an intense, frenzied manner will make you appear immature.

-       Jot down short notes during adverse testimony, so that when it is your turn to give your own case-in-chief you will not forget to clarify important issues.

# OVERVIEW OF CASE-IN-CHIEF

Both sides will make an opening statement to the judge, identifying their issues, outlining their evidence, and indicating what orders will be requested. Upon completion of the opening statements, the moving party presents their case-in-chief evidence through witnesses. Order of witnesses, and evidence presentation is a tactical decision that can have tremendous significance.

Each witness takes the stand, swears in, and is then directly questioned by the attorney. Questioning usually begins with preliminary information about the witness and their personal connection with the case. Strict legal procedures govern the type and manner of questioning allowed for a witness.

The general rules during testimony are:

- Questions calling for narrative answers are used in the direct examination.

- Leading questions are used in cross-examination.

A trial judge has much discretion about whether to allow certain questions to be answered by a witness. This includes self-serving statements made out of court. The judge is guided by very complicated laws and rules regarding evidence presentation.

After direct examination of a witness, cross-examination is allowed. The purpose of the cross-examination is to bring out favorable facts, expose deficiencies, establish any bias, or impeach a witness. Cross-examination is limited to areas covered in direct examination. Redirect examination follows completion of the direct examination. This back and forth continues until knowledge of the witness is completed.

Once the moving party "rests," then the responding party presents their evidence. After the responding party "rests," the moving party is allowed to rebut. The process then goes back to the other side for sur-rebuttle. This back and forth process will continue until each side has exhausted all questioning.

After both sides have "rested," the attorneys give their final argument and the matter is submitted for a decision. Some judges will make immediate decisions, others will take the matter under "submission" and send out a written ruling to the attorneys.

## APPEALS - POST-TRIAL MOTIONS

***Appeals and Post-Trial Motions*** are available to the losing party. Appellate court judges rarely overturn the trial judge in the custody battle as they only see the papers and not the people.

## THE ULTIMATE DECISION

The courtroom is your field of battle, like a football field on Super Bowl Sunday. You are now in the "big leagues."

You must prepare for your court hearing as though it is the most important game of your life.

At the conclusion of the court hearing, you want to hear the voice of the judge say the magic words.....

## *CUSTODY TO FATHER*

# CHAPTER 9

# HANDLING YOURSELF IN COURT

In sports, before expecting to win any games, a player must learn the rules, practices the basics, and develop strategies. You use this same approach to win in court. Learn the court rules outlined herein, as even the attorneys do not know all the obscure court rules. Practice the basics outlined herein by video taping and role playing in front of a mirror or with friends. Stick with the strategies used by fathers who have already won custody. You do not have the time to experiment through trial and error, and the risk is great.

Your fieldtrips to family law courtrooms will allow you to watch custody cases in progress, and observe the personality of individual judges. You will note a wide range of behavior in the litigants and it will become very apparent as to what works and what does not work in the courtroom. You do not want to irritate your judge by well meaning, but inappropriate conduct.

A court hearing moves along rapidly, and is conducted according to rules that can be very confusing. Knowing the rules of a court hearing, and how to conduct yourself within those rules, will give you an incredible advantage. Fathers properly "prepped," have a distinct edge. Your concentration should be focusing on strategizing rather than making mistakes in courtroom etiquette. The stakes are high and you want to perform well.

A good way to learn courtroom etiquette is to rent movies with lots of courtroom action and watch them with the sound turned off. Your attention will focus on body language used and the great impact of this communication format. You will quickly learn to figure out what is going on from the actor's body language although you are not hearing the words. Court orders will greatly affect your life and can take years to turn around. Professional athletes stick with what has worked for other athletes, you must do likewise in court.

## BASIC DO'S AND DON'T'S

There is behavior that is unacceptable in sports and there is behavior that is unacceptable in the courtroom. Knowing basic do's and don'ts in courtroom etiquette are what will set you apart from the average litigant.

Minor violations of court etiquette and protocol will not damage your position all that much. However, an accumulation of infractions could affect the judge's opinion of you, and this could be devastating. To avoid violations of courtroom etiquette, we have developed a list of common mistakes made by litigants. The following basic do's and don'ts should become second nature to you.

## BASIC DO'S

**DO:** Leave for your day in court early, to allow time for handling unforeseen problems such as traffic congestion and parking problems.

**DO:** Call the courtroom if you are going to be late, as courtroom staff will not answer the telephone during calendar call. Get the direct phone number ahead of time.

**DO:** Pay a visit to the restroom to, among other things, check out personal appearance.

**DO:** Check the calendar posted outside the courtroom, as it will give you an indication of the sequential order in which your case will be heard.

**DO:** Check in with the bailiff, and inform him/her of your presence and order of appearance.

**DO:** Take a seat in the courtroom and be very respectful of ongoing court proceedings prior to your own.

**DO:** Pay close attention to how the judge conducts court business and note individual idiosyncrasies of the judge.

## BASIC DO NOT'S

**DO NOT:** Drink alcoholic beverages for twenty-four (24) hours prior to the court hearing. Any stress induced sweat will make you reek of alcohol.

**DO NOT:** Carry anything metal: A pocket knife, scissors, or any other metal objects that will set off the courthouse metal detectors.

**DO NOT:** Chew gum, wear a hat, read the newspaper, or display disrespectful conduct while waiting for your case number to be called.

**DO NOT:** Take a beeper, cellular phone, or any other noise-making device into the courtroom.

**DO NOT:** Leave the courtroom for any reason without checking with the bailiff.

**DO NOT:** Walk in the "well." This is the area between the council table and the judge's bench.

**DO NOT:** Give documents or photographs directly to the judge, instead, hand them directly to the bailiff. Have copies available for the opposition.

## QUESTION AND ANSWER FORMAT

Evidence presented to a judge is given through a question and answer format. A short speech is allowed at the beginning of the court hearing and is called an *opening statement*. This opening statement is a roadmap for the judge to follow. Another short speech is allowed at the conclusion of the court hearing which summarizes the most important issues of the case and is called, a *final argument*. Between opening speeches and closing speeches, a question and answer format is followed.

Judges get very upset when litigants give mini-speeches throughout their testimony, as testimony is intended to gather facts and not to make arguments. A witness attempting to give speeches during testimony, might be viewed as a non-responsive witness; someone who is avoiding questions thereby giving the appearance of being evasive, and untruthful.

Certain questions asked in court will call for an objection, which requires the judge to make a ruling on whether the question is legally permissible. Once you have heard the objection, wait until the judge's ruling before answering the question. Attempting to respond before or during the judge's ruling is a major mistake. The answer will be stricken, and you will have upset the judge. A series of violations will adversely affect your entire testimony.

Objections that are *sustained,* do not require an answer. Objections that are *denied,* do require an answer.

**Note:** An objection to a question being asked, sends out a signal that the question is of great significance, and is an alarm bell for you to pay close attention to the question being asked.

# USE COURT TIME WISELY

Court hearings are conducted extremely quickly and have far reaching consequences. You do not want to make mistakes in court, nor waste precious time on irrelevant issues. You are given a specified time period in court in which to present your story, and cannot afford to waste time on irrelevant matters.

At the commencement of a court hearing, a judge will ask about the following two areas:

**Controverted Issues:** The judge will ask what issues are involved and evidence will be limited those specific issues. Testimony on other issues will not be allowed.

**Time Estimate:** The judge will set a specified time period for the court hearing and then enforce time allotted. Going over the time estimate can result in a mistrial.

A mistrial can be declared when the court hearing is not concluded within the time allotted. A litigant not finishing within the time limit, is disapprovingly viewed upon by the judge as this court time could have been use for another case. A mistrial means starting over again, waiting for another day in court. You may find yourself in a situation where you have to set priorities, cut to the chase, and make time adjustments to avoid a mistrial.

The time estimate given to a judge for a court hearing is calculated by the number of witnesses and length of their stories. The time is then added up and a time estimate decided. Multiple witnesses on the same facts are cumulative and judges do not have the time to hear the same facts made by several different people. Select the most credible witnesses.

## MAJOR PROBLEMS FIRST

A judge's time is limited, and only so much time can be given to any one case, therefore, you must set priorities. Prepare a priority list and use it to help you remember the issues. Start with the most important issues first and then move on to the other problems in descending order of significance.

Judges begin with major problems first as there is rarely enough time in court to hear all the relevant facts of a case. It is impossible for anyone to accurately prioritize their own problems because of inherent inability to have an objective, unimpassioned view of events. Discuss your situation with family members and close friends to get a variety of opinions and viewpoints on your personal situation.

## TIMING YOUR PUNCHES

Timing is critical in all of life particularly in a courtroom setting. In court, as in all of life, the timing of a statement can be decisive and more impacting than the statement itself. Watch the judge closely for the critical-moment when he/she becomes more alert and pays extra attention to the testimony being given. Judges telegraph this critical-moment by facial gestures, and turning directly to observe the witness. This critical-moment is the time for you to turn, face the judge, lower your voice, and continue giving favorable information until the judge looks bored.

Timing Is Critical
**WHEN**
Can Be More Effective Than
**WHAT**

Learn how to think like a judge. The only way to do this is to take a fieldtrip to the court house and observe custody cases in action. Notice how many litigants are not being responsive to questions being asked. The metaphor, *"You're talking apples, I'm talking oranges,"* is an example of disorganized communication. In court, communication must center on what the judge wants to talk about.

A non-responsive litigant, refusing to stay on point, causes confusion and is a waste of court time. Bombardment of rambling testimony on different issues, is ineffective and not helpful to the judge. Give your facts in small sound bytes as opposed to long rambling dissertations.

It Is Just As Important To Know

**WHEN *NOT TO SAY* SOMETHING**

As It Is To Know

**WHEN *TO SAY* SOMETHING**

Speaking at the right moment requires a sense of timing and good judgment. If the opportunity arises for you to make an important point to the judge, and it is not being received with your sense of importance, back off and wait for a more appropriate moment to make your point.

**Note:** Judges let the person losing do more talking, as he/she wants to give the person every chance to present all evidence. The person talking the most, is generally losing.

Good timing requires good judgment. Constant evaluation and assessment must be ongoing during a court hearing such as: How much time is left, what issues need clarification, which matters still must be brought up, all of which are subjective decisions resulting in time management. You will have to make decisions on which facts to leave out to have sufficient time for more important matters.

Managing your time in court requires setting priorities; sort out the most important issues and leave the less important ones until after the major events are covered. When on a fieldtrip, you will see how some fathers get right to the important issues of their case in a clear and concise manner, while other fathers are floundering through the issues. **Learn by example.**

When a litigant testifies in an unfocused manner, the judge has a more difficult time in understanding the dynamics of the situation. It is hard for a judge to help solve a problem when he/she does not understand the point a litigant is trying to make.

Don't Lose Sight Of The Reason You Are In Court

\*\*\*

### *"In The Best Interest Of The Children"*

You want the judge to accurately assess your parenting abilities. This can be done by making your concerns clear and on point. Then, move on to your next point. You do not want to overload the judge with too much information or disorganized facts. Information delivered to the judge should be timed with short sound bytes.

# IMAGE MANAGEMENT

Appearance has always counted in the courtroom. A judge begins observing and assessing litigants from the very moment they enter his/her courtroom by taking mental note of a litigants:

- Clothes.
- Hair style.
- Body language.
- Facial expressions.
- Demeanor.
- Eye movement.
- Posture.

Go into the courtroom well before the commencement of your court hearing. This will allow the judge to evaluate your demeanor. The judge conducts an evaluation of the audience in a discrete manner, oftentimes out of the corner of his/her eye. conduct yourself as if you are in church.

Judges do not have time to know each litigant well. Judges begin making mental evaluations about a litigant from the minute they walk into the courtroom. Your image in court should always project a person who is courteous and respectful. All judges have preconceived ideas of how a person should act in court.

You are constantly being watched around the courthouse and in the courtroom. Most family law courthouses have hidden video cameras and audio surveillance for every room in the court building, restrooms, parking structure, hallways, etc. Consider yourself being videotaped at all times.

Anyone seen using obscene gestures, shouting, glaring, or showing other weird conduct in and around the courthouse, will be watched by security staff. It will not help your case if your are under close surveillance by security guards as it will project a negative perception about your case.

Judges are aware that attorneys caution their clients to act in control when in the courtroom. Judges also know a person's behavior can be obnoxious outside the courtroom. Some judges roam the halls, incognito, looking for litigants who are acting irresponsible, in an attempt to identify problem cases. Other judges have their bailiff and staff keep them informed of litigants who are displaying strange or unusual behavior. The lesson for you is not to appear obstreperous (boisterous, disorderly, loud, unruly), but to look like an upstanding citizen. If you quack like a duck, waddle like a duck, and look like a duck, then you can't fault a judge for thinking you are a duck.

Here are some practical tips you can use to increase your credibility and believability when in court.

## 1.    Dressing for Court:

Appearance is always important in the courtroom, and litigants are often coached by their attorneys on how they should dress. Credibility is the reason for a dress code as you may not be taken seriously with improper attire. Dress conservatively and have a neat haircut as you want the judge to concentrate on you, not on what you are wearing. If you have a job that requires a work uniform, wear it to court. Your work uniform will visually indicate to the judge the level of your responsibility.

## 2.    Honesty and Credibility:

Honesty and credibility are characteristics that result in believability. An honest person will admit when they have made a mistake, even if it causes them embarrassment or humiliation. Honesty is an admirable quality separating a principled person with integrity, from a person with selective memory using half truths.

Honesty is used as a "benchmark" by the judge to give weight to an individual's testimony. A judge will not differentiate between a big lie and a little lie, both are dishonest. Therefore, when a judge catches someone in a lie (big or small), then everything said by that person is suspect. Being caught in a little white lie places doubt on everything said. A person's credibility is also damaged if testimony is evasive or non-responsive.

Being honest and looking honest are separate and distinct. You see it every day on television, where the actors are speaking lines, not telling the truth, yet appearing believable. There are times when a person is telling the truth, but appear untruthful because of nervousness, eye movement, hesitancy, etc.

Effective listening requires more than just making eye contact with the witness. Nonverbal acknowledgment through facial gestures, head nodding and body movements can politely indicate to the judge that you are not in agreement with what is being said. However, overusage of these nonverbal techniques is annoying, disruptive, and will be viewed as an immature attempt to sway the judge. Proper use of body language to communicate disbelief will alert the judge that this is an important area that may need clarification to trap the liar.

3.    **Converse Visually:**

People communicate in two ways:

## VISUALLY + AUDIBLY

All females are astute at communicating both visually and audibly which they learned from other females while growing up and hanging out with other females. Conversely, most males only use the audible method of communication and are not skilled at projecting their thoughts through body language. Males are taught to use restrained body language and stay in physical control. An out of control male is considered a real danger, yet a female out of control is not. Most males do not communicate their emotions through use of body language. Therefore, they have to make a really conscious effort to converse visually. Males can learn to use body language to communicate their feelings to the judge when someone else is testifying, however, they must be more reserved in this method of communication than females.

**Note:** Females communicate by using two channels of communication, sight and sound, thereby input more information than males.

Judges gather information with their ears and eyes. Some are more audible, while others are more visual.

## EAR or EYE

You will not know if your judge is more impacted by ear or eye until you have taken the time to observe his/her actions for a while, so appeal to both senses - sight and sound.

## 4.     Eye Contact:

The eyes are the windows to the soul. The degree of eye opening can be quite telling. Keep eye contact with your judge, hold that eye contact, and let the judge see into your soul.

The judge watches everyone from the moment they come into his/her courtroom; whether on the witness stand, at the council table, or in the audience. Judges are interested in the reaction of a litigant to opposing testimony. How you use your eyes when reacting to something said, can be more enlightening to a judge than the information being given. Eye movement is how you communicate disturbing testimony.

It is all right to occasionally roll your eyes or give a slight grimace to show your disagreement with what is being said, but use caution and do not over do it. Using too many facial gestures or too much body language will be viewed as immature and over acting.

Communicating through eye movement is very important and can be learned. Use a mirror and pay special attention to your eyes. Pay particular attention to the different effects obtained by:

- Squinting.
- Blinking.
- Staring.
- Open wide.

On your fieldtrips to the courthouse, watch for the visual communication going on between the judge, court staff, attorneys, and litigants. You can learn to decipher what is being said visually.

### 5.    Effective Body Language:

A female expresses body language much more effectively than a male. Watch a female from across a crowded room and observe the ease in which she expresses herself. In court, females will use their body language very effectively to add emphasis and to convey displeasure. Females have the option to bring things to a screeching halt, by crying on cue.

Judges also use body language. Judges will nonverbally communicate to court staff, control attorney conduct, register disapproval, and let the witness know when they have made their point. This body language is conveniently not on the record.

Knowing that females are going to use body language in court, knowing judges, staff, and attorneys are going to use body language in court, it only makes sense that you should learn to use body language also. Effective body language can be learned.

Body language is used in three distinct ways:

- To show respect for the court.

- To put "spin" on your testimony.

- To indicate something is askew.

You can learn all three techniques by studying actors in courtroom dramas on TV or at the movies. Watch the different body language used by both males/females. You will notice how this method of communication is perceived differently, depending on the actor's gender, male/female.

Males overusing body language can ruin the effectiveness of the technique. It is acceptable for a male to show displeasure by using minor gestures, but they must be very subtle. Restrained hand movements, lifted eye brows, a slight shaking of the head, a roll of the eyes, and leaning forward are acceptable gestures for a male to use in court.

> **Note:** When you are listening to adverse testimony, be careful not to overuse visual communication. Every little movement you make will be noticed by the judge even though he/she may not acknowledge such moves.

Proper body language calls for calm, relaxed, confident appearance. Appearing disgruntled, hyperactive, argumentative, all are improper impressions to convey to a judge. You will come across negatively to the judge if you:

- Interrupt a witness.
- Make faces.
- Wave your arms.
- Pull on your attorney's sleeve.
- Scribble notes furiously.
- Incessant whispering.

All of the above behavior is considered unacceptable in a court of law. Inappropriate conduct only makes you look out of control, immature, and unable to cope with stressful situations. The judge will be surreptitiously monitoring your conduct by his/her peripheral vision. So, sit back, relax, and keep your lips zipped until it is your turn to give your side of the story.

## 6.    Inappropriate Behavior:

A good maneuver used at the wrong time has no effect and can be counterproductive. It is very important that you appear sensitive when mom is telling her side of the story. This will project maturity on your part. The judge will be interested in your reactions to mom's testimony and watching closely for negative responses. You will have a chance to counter mom's comments when it is your turn to talk.

Smirking when mom uses crocodile tears will be seen as cruel and insensitive. Yet, smirking at another point in testimony might be an appropriate visual rebuttal. Well-intended actions can come across in an entirely different way if used at the wrong time. Think long and hard before using any excessive body movement.

**Note:** When mom is testifying and using histrionics to add emphasis to her story, do not smirk; instead, get the judges eye and hold your eye contact without any facial gestures.

All males in a family law courtroom are suspect. Staff and security personnel watch very closely for the "wounded rhinoceros," a regular psychopath in the family law courts. Males are scrutinized until court staff is satisfied that the individual is in control. Upon entering the courtroom, take a seat, respectfully listen to the ongoing proceedings, and behave yourself. In the courtroom, low whispering only. If you need to continue a conversation outside the courtroom, request permission from the bailiff. Discourteous conduct will reflect negatively upon you.

## 7.    10 - Minute Speech:

When the time comes to tell your story, you must have prepared, rehearsed, and memorized a 10-minute speech on your version of the most important events. Condensing one's lifestyle down into ten minutes is a difficult task and will require help from a friend, to get an impartial, dispassionate viewpoint. Write down your thoughts, set priorities, condense your issues, and practice your delivery in front of a mirror or video camera.

This 10-minute speech should be delivered clearly and concisely. Make it easy for the judge to follow your reasoning and understand your thinking. Start with recent events and work backwards as judges are more interested in the current situation. Memorizing your 10-minute speech will ensure that all major problems are brought to the attention of the judge and that nothing critical is left out.

The human dynamics of warring parents are repetitive, therefore, judges begin to pigeonhole the case as the story unfolds. If you have prepared, rehearsed, and memorized your 10-minute speech, you have a better chance of being placed in the right pigeonhole. Set your family situation apart from the average garden-variety custody case, custody to mom, visitation to dad. Your 10-minute speech must include the following:

- Identify major issues.
- Present events clearly.
- Give facts, not conclusions.

All great politicians and salespersons have "canned" speeches, and you should too. A well-prepared speech will free your mind to handle the mid-course changes and surprises that occur in family law court.

Your time in court is priceless, you must prepare by:

1. **YOU MUST:** Use your discretion in determining what issues to bring up that will be most helpful in getting your point across.

2. **YOU MUST:** Appear honest and show credibility so you are one of those 10% of winning cases in which dad is given custody.

3. **YOU MUST:** Tailor your presentation so the case will be considered unique and different from the average garden-variety custody battle whereby mom wins.

4. **YOU MUST:** Keep all discussions targeted on the major issues, those that will have an effect on the outcome of who wins custody.

5. **YOU MUST:** Not waste your precious court time on issues that are irrelevant and have no bearing on the custodial decision.

6. **YOU MUST:** Memorize a 10-minute narrative of the major facts of your story so your delivery is clear, concise, and with conviction.

## SELL YOURSELF

Think of yourself as a product, and begin your sales presentation the minute you pull into the courthouse parking lot. Consider yourself on constant exhibition when on the courthouse grounds. Try to appear relaxed, alert, and in total control. Do not overreact. Don't quarrel with mom or her witnesses and keep your own witnesses from doing likewise. Be polite and courteous to everyone, you never know who will be riding in the elevator with you. You want to look like everybody else. This is not the time to wear your favorite Hawaiian shirt. Look around the courthouse on one of your fieldtrips and notice the fathers that stand out and how the bailiffs pay close attention to these males.

Dressing in a coat and tie, shows your respect for the judicial system. A neatly pressed work uniform is acceptable, and can indicate that you are capable of meaningful employment and have responsible duties. Litigants who come to court unshaven, with greasy finger nails, wearing unpressed clothes, and having unorganized papers, look like they cannot handle themselves, let alone a child.

First Impressions Are Lasting Impressions!

Lack of preparation is the greatest single reason for a father losing in court. A father that wants to win custody must be prepared before he can play smart, hard, and fair. A courtroom field of battle can change and shift directions quickly. Therefore, you must be ready to make immediate adjustments in order to handle sudden surprises. Stick with proven strategies and tactics that have been successful for other fathers. You must believe in your cause to sell your cause.

# CHAPTER 10

# THE JUDGE

Judges like snowflakes, are one of a kind, each an original. Consequences of your experience with snowflakes can vary from:

Buried Alive In A Blizzard

to

Pleasure Skiing In Aspen

Your experience in the courtroom can be just as varied. You must prepare for your meeting a judge with the same thoroughness that you would use in planning a trip to the snow country. Hope for the best, ready for a blizzard.

Fathers embroiled in a custody battle need to have a basic understanding of the job responsibilities of a judge. Being aware of what judges can, and cannot do, will allow you to concentrate on areas where the judge can make a difference.

For a father to do well in court, he needs to know the character traits common to all judges, and understand the judicial thought process. Knowing what arguments influence a judge's thinking, will allow you to focus your presentation on what has worked for winning fathers. Learning about judges is serious business, and is essential in order to design a strategy that will be successful with the judge handling your case.

A family law judge made a profound statement when he said to warring parents, *"I am now a member of your family, I sit at the head of the table, and from this point on, I, will be making all of the decisions as to the lives of your children."*

Society has delegated awesome responsibilities to family law judges over the lives of children. Your judge will make decisions that will change the course of you and your children's lives. Therefore, knowledge of a judge's role in the custody battle will be of great help to you in keeping on the same wavelength as your judge. The more you know about how judges go about doing their jobs, the more effective you will be when interacting with your individual judge.

**Note:** If you want to learn about giraffes, you would go to the zoo, therefore, it makes sense, if you want to learn about judges you must go to the courthouse and watch family law judges in action.

# JUDICIAL DEMEANOR

All judges have similar personality traits and common characteristics. Individuals elected to the position of a judicial officer will have a thought process similar to other judges. The task of learning about judges is not that difficult, because judges, like birds, flock together. As a group, judges are about as alike as a flock of seagulls. Judges strive to be consistent, so don't be thinking that one judge will turn North, when the flock is flying South.

Once you have an understanding of the judicial thought process, you can begin studying the individual judge who will be *"sitting at the head of your table."* Adjustments can then be made to work with the judge hearing your case.

The way for you to handle the specific judge assigned to your case is:

- Learn the character traits common to all judges.

- Study specific mannerisms, personality, and quirks of the judge who will hear your case.

Judges work in courtrooms that are open to the public. Take a day off from work, sit in a family law courtroom, and watch what goes on. This fieldtrip to your local courthouse will educate you beyond your wildest dreams. Keep in mind that your "court-watching" will be noticed, and judges have the memory of an elephant. So, be courteous, respectful, and polite, you may someday find yourself in front of that same judge.

# JUDICIAL POWER

Judges are empowered with authority to make decisions that dispense justice. Their authority comes from the United States Constitution, by which the judiciary has been established as a separate and equal branch of our government. The symbol for justice, is a blindfolded woman wearing a black robe and holding a scale, This symbol represents the trust in an individual who has been given the honor of serving as a judge.

## THE SYMBOL FOR JUSTICE IS A WOMAN:

Wearing a blindfold - symbolizing equality.

Wearing a black robe - representing impartiality.

Holding a scale - balancing both sides of a story.

Judges are government officials, with the power to decide questions in controversy. Judges take pride in the high position they have attained and have big egos. Judges are not prejudiced, but do have set opinions based on individual life experiences. Judges are closely monitored by a judicial council, and complaints filed on a judge will be thoroughly investigated.

Spend at least three full days watching the judges that run your local family courthouse so that you will know what to expect when your day in court arrives. The more you know about the individual judge handling your case, the better your chance of influencing his/her decisions.

## REFEREE IN A BLACK ROBE

In olden days, the judge wore a wig and black robe, to visually demonstrate impartiality. The wool wig is the source of an old saying, *"Quit trying to pull the wool over my eyes."* The old-fashioned way for a judge to tell someone to, *"knock off the bullshit."* Human character traits and frailties have not changed over the years, and judges still hear litigants that:

- Omit important facts.
- Misrepresent events.
- Apply "spin" to stories.
- Selective memories.
- Tell outright lies.

A judge once stated, *"A courtroom is like a computer, completely neutral, crap in means crap out."* This comment is meant to emphasize the importance of your making worthwhile contributions to get valuable output. You are in control of your own destiny. It is up to you to package your story in a way that will influence the judge in your favor.

Family law judges take the bench each day and hear wildly different versions of the same events. These conflicting accounts are told by equally credible witnesses, and there is just no way each version could have occurred. This leaves judges in a position of continuously trying to figure out which version of events is more accurate. A judge is the referee in a courtroom. Judges, like referees, know the rules, remain neutral, and try to make fair calls. Judgment calls are made in the heat of the contest and decisions are made based on knowledge, experience and perception.

Bad calls are bound to happen in court, as in sports, and this is when the maturity level of players is noted by the referee. The mature, responsible, player abides by the bad call and gets on with the game. You should handle bad decisions in court the same way you would respond in a sporting event. Know that a bad call can be overcome. Reacting with unsportsmanlike conduct will hurt you more than the damage of the bad call.

The judge will be making decisions that will shape the future lives of your children and some bad calls are to be expected. A mature response to a bad call projects an excellent sportsmanlike image. Determinations made by a judge are life shaping and will establish a child's destiny:

**WHO:** Will live in the same house.

**WHAT:** School will be attended.

**WHEN:** They will see the other parent.

**WHERE:** They will reside.

**HOW:** Holidays will be spent.

**ETC. - ETC. - ETC.**

A family law court judge, a total stranger, will be making decisions normally decided by ones parents. This power to set a child's life in place is taken very seriously. Like referees, judges make the best decision based on what they have seen and heard, then move on to the next case, not looking back.

## THEATRICS VIEWED BY A JUDGE

Adventures in a family law courtroom are unlike anything you will ever encounter on this planet. Each courtroom is run a bit differently. There are no juries. Average people are in emotional overload, and the stakes are astronomically high for all involved. The individual in charge, a family law judge, looks out each morning to a courtroom filled with litigants and witnesses stressed to the limit of human endurance. Judges handling family law cases put up with litigants yelling, swearing, name-calling, and making threats. Tension often escalates into physical violence. In the stress measurements of life, a hostile divorce is at the very top.

Family law judges deal with repeating human problems with male and female discord that has been going on since Adam and Eve. Your story is not anything new, only a different twist on recurring problems. Judges think they have seen it all, and have worked out formula solutions for the repeating human dramas. Adultery is a topic brought repeatedly before the court. Cheating is the common thread, only technology and partners change:

- X-rated motels have replaced cars in drive-in theaters replacing buggies under covered bridges.

- Sex villain can be a relative, best friend, neighbor, co-worker, or maybe another woman.

Society no longer punishes the sin of adultery. Dueling is illegal, you can't shoot the bastard, or even sue him. Humiliation caused by adultery cannot be fixed in a court of law. Judges do not want to hear the sordid details. This wrong will only be righted in the hereafter.

The "fog of war" hovering over family law courtrooms is predictable to the judicial officers as they see the same madness only different players. During your fieldtrip to the courthouse, you will notice a rhythm in each courtroom that moves to the beat of the judge. You will observe how some fathers do well, some fathers come close, and some fathers fail miserably. It will become obvious when watching the court proceedings, which fathers have done their homework and are prepared for their day in court. Watch how much easier it is for a judge to make decisions when working with fathers that are well organized and prepared.

You can help make the judge's work a lot easier if you are clear and concise in your presentation. Categorize your problems and then give them to the judge by:

**First:**          Concisely stating your issues.

**Second:**          Providing specific examples.

Deliver the facts by concisely stating the issues in your case, then provide specific examples for the judge. This allows him/her to evaluate the situation without spending a lot of time digging for the factual information. The better picture you provide for the judge, the more likely you will be placed in the right pigeonhole.

Do not give a long, rambling account of mom's insults to you, as this will be perceived by the judge as complaints coming from disgruntled dumpee. Do not confuse the judge with topics that are inflammatory and the judge has no interest in.

# JUDICIAL BIAS

Fathers involved in a custody battle must be realistic and accept the fact that judges, like other human beings, have developed personal attitudes, outlooks, and opinions locked into his/her way of thinking. This is called, *judicial bias*. The word bias means one has leanings either in favor of or against something or someone. When the word bias is used with a judge, this thought process must not be confused with the negative word, *prejudice*. A judge works hard to keep opinions private and totally out of the judicial process but draws upon personal experiences in two areas:

## Determining
## Who Is Telling The Truth

### then

## Drafting Orders
## To Fix The Situation

## 1.     Determining Who Is Telling The Truth:

The judge will rely upon life experiences to help determine which parent is telling the truth. Judges have very inquisitive minds. Over the years thousands of people go though a courtroom and judges acquire an encyclopedic knowledge about the ways of the world. You will note a judge asking a witness about something that is totally irrelevant to the case but of interest to him/her. Expect your judge to be quite knowledgeable about your areas of expertise. Always be truthful.

Tell the whole truth about everything. A witness that misstates or exaggerates the truth about a peripheral issue is not going to be believed about any statement made. Your being honest even when embarrassing will enhance your credibility. Dishonest statements about peripheral issues will damage your believability and you won't be believed when you are telling the truth.

**Note:** A judge may have once worked in an auto repair shop and knows how long it takes to repair a tire. A father saying it takes four hours to change a flat tire is not going to be believed when he tells the judge he prepares all the meals for his children.

## 2.    Drafting Orders To Fit The Situation:

Judges use personal experiences and 20/20 hindsight when making future orders to solve reoccurring problems. Family law judges get together at events, and exchange solutions to repeating problems. The standardized solutions are then modified to fit individual situations.

Learn the standard solutions implemented by the judge assigned to your case by, respectfully sitting in his/her courtroom, talking with other fathers, and attending meetings of local fathers rights groups. Exchange of information on judicial inclinations is very valuable and needs constant updating.

**Note:** If a judge routinely orders first right of babysitting to the other parent, make the request. Information on a judge's judicial leanings should be passed on to others.

## QUESTIONABLE TESTIMONY

A judge in criminal law goes to work and deals with:

### Bad People Acting Their Best

A judge in family law goes to work and deals with:

### Good People Acting Their Worst

The *bailiff* (courtroom security) in a family law court writes more contact incident reports in a month, than the jail bailiff does in a year. Emotions run high and memories become selective. The wonderful times are forgotten and the hard times are thrown up. Judges are well aware of the stressors in their own courtroom and the questionable testimony that occurs.

The intricate equation of "truth-seeking," is a difficult job for a judge. When watching a court hearing in progress, try to figure out in your own mind who is telling the truth. Your experience will emphasize how difficult the job is for a judge in trying to get an accurate picture of what is really happening. The job of being a judge is not easy. A judge comes to work every day and must wade through:

- Self-serving statements.
- Different versions.
- Sharp attorneys.
- Hysterical parents.
- Biased witnesses.
- Long, complicated stories.
- Limited court time.
- Bald-faced liars.

While you are watching evidence being presented in court, ask yourself these two questions:

*"What do I believe?"*

*"What would I do as the judge?"*

The primary responsibility of a judge in our society, is to resolve questions in controversy. This is simple to state, but a very difficult task, because of the human elements involved.

Confusion arises about what is really occurring in a family situation and a judge has to deal with this confusion daily. Often, both parents truly believe their story is accurate. This requires the judge to sift through conflicting facts and make determinations by using his/her personal knowledge, experience and perceptions.

## TRAITS COMMON TO ALL JUDGES

Every occupation requires certain personality traits to do a job well and this includes the job of being a judge. A listing of all the traits that would help a person do a better job as a judge would end up looking like the Boy Scout oath: Prudent, methodical, high integrity, sound reasoning, conscientious, decent, impartial, etc. A listing of honorable characteristics will not be helpful to you in analyzing a particular judge, however, there are four common traits to all judges you must learn before you can begin to interact with the judge handling your case.

*INTELLIGENT - FAIR - WISE - FIRM*

1. **INTELLIGENT:** Judges are extremely clever and savvy. Therefore, don't get too comfortable with a judge that takes a laid-back approach. A judge might be using this technique as a way to ferret out the truth - giving you just enough rope to hang yourself. Judges know the law, so do not waste your time going to the law library in an attempt to get through law school in a weekend. Spend as much time as you can packaging the facts of your case so that your judge gets an accurate picture of the actual events. The hardest job for judges is to figure out which parent to believe. Once the facts of the case have been presented, a judge will make decisions based on what he/she believes, and then apply the correct law. Let the judge be in charge of knowing the law; they have extensive educational background in family law and what they need from you is facts and information that can be applied to the law.

2. **FAIR:** Judges try to be extremely fair. Judges will go out of the way to be fair and to appear fair. Parents will obey and cooperate with judicial orders when made by a fair and impartial judge. Judges know how important your court appearance means to you, and will bend over backwards to give you a fair hearing. Providing, you behave yourself. Boisterous, rude, and insolent behavior will provoke the wrath of the judge and then fairness will be dispensed sharply. You will be given an opportunity to tell the judge important facts of your case and enough time to respond to mom's version of events. However, you will not have time to tell your life story. The judge only wants to know sufficient facts to make a fair decision.

3. **WISE:** Judges are undeniably wise. They have refined their ability to sort out the important information from the muddle of facts presented. This wisdom is a learned trait that is always being updated. Unique facts will get extra consideration from a judge, however, it is up to you to convince him/her of your special situation. Judges are continuously dealing with imperfect people trying their best and it takes wisdom to sort through the pettiness, revenge, and anger of a custody battle. Acrimony lingers over all custody litigation and it is your job to appear as if you are not the hostile individual. Be truthful, candid, and direct when giving testimony even if it means admitting a mistake. Your being honest about a past mistake and expressing remorse shows you are taking pro-active measures to overcome the problem. Let the judge decide the weight of your mistake. Denial or rationalization can be worse than the actual offense itself.

4. **FIRM:** Judges have the responsibility to maintain order in the court and the streets. They listen to explanations of antisocial behavior and then make decisions that will punish the offender and prevent further occurrences. Judges are not easily persuaded to give second chances. This firmness is a required personality trait of a judge and should not be taken too personally. All litigants must contend with stern judges. Tell your version of events in a forthright and respectful manner. Every father involved in a court hearing faces the same pressure. The strength of your conviction and your unwavering persistence will give credibility to both you and your story.

Judges have lots of character traits in common, but the four most important traits are: An *intelligent* judge who knows family law well, tries hard to be *fair* to both sides, makes *wise* decisions based on facts presented, and takes *firm* action when obdurate behavior is used by either party. You can learn to work with a judge by appealing to his/her:

## *Intelligence - Fairness - Wisdom - Firmness*

The four traits listed fall into specific areas that you can work to your advantage. Keep in mind, judges are high-powered individuals who often move up to higher positions in society. Judges are highly talented individuals, want to make a difference in this world, and, don't get paid very much. A person with the same skills in private industry makes about double the income. Judges are in it out of sense of patriotic duty. The money is not the motivation for people who agree to take on the responsibilities of a judgeship. Judges are motivated by public service, strive to maintain order in the families before them, and have a strong desire to make positive changes in peoples lives.

The other common personality traits of individual judges range from: Courteous to rude, slow to impatient, compassionate to unsympathetic, and will not affect the decisions made in your case. Judges are human, have individual personality flaws but such traits will not affect the outcome of your case. If you have done your homework, made fieldtrips to your local courthouse, you know the personality idiosyncrasies of the various judges. After studying these judges, you will know what irritates them, how their courtroom is run, the preferences, and other quirks so that you can do what works and avoid what doesn't work.

## INDIVIDUAL JUDGES

There is an old attorney saying:

*"I don't care what the law says, I want to know who the judge is."*

Each family law judge has an individual personality and has arrived on the bench through a circuitous route of life experiences. This personal history plays into the mindset of your individual judge. Past experiences with family interactions will influence a judge, and orders will be made to solve reoccurring problems as they revolve through the courtroom door. Then, adjustments are then made to fine-tune orders to fit each case. Judicial solutions are designed on a trial and error basis. A judge listens to the evidence, he/she mentally sorts through the facts, categorizes the problems, and applies standard solutions. Problem identification is crucial as these judicial solutions pigeonhole your case.

A tragedy will occur if your case is misdiagnosed and the wrong prescription is handed out. A wrong solution ordered by the judge will place you in the wrong pigeonhole. You do not want to be put into the wrong pigeonhole as a wrong solution can take years to turn around. Make sure that your family situation is accurately differentiated from the average custody case that calls for a standard solution of custody to mom and visitation to dad.

Identify the key issues of your case, those areas which you want to bring before the judge. Visit your local law library and look in the index of a book on family law for your issues. The purpose of reading about your issues is to get insight into the thought process of judicial thinking, not to learn complicated areas of the law.

**Note:** There is always an inherent danger of lay persons misreading or misinterpreting a legal text, so do not get caught up in the legalese. The purpose for you going to the law library is to learn the judicial thought process and not to get confused with complicated legal terms.

Law libraries have background information on the local judges. Ask the librarian to assist you in finding biographical information on your judge, make photocopies, and study the profile. There are two distinct types of judicial personalities:

1. **Type "A" Personality:** This type "A" personality judge is an abrupt, fast, hard driving individual who can come across as discourteous and rude. You are probably aware of this kind of personality from school, work, or family. This no-nonsense type of person wants to get to the major issues immediately and fix the problems, ASAP. This personality type must be handled cautiously as the mind speed can result in errors. If you antagonize or upset this individual, you can easily end up in the wrong pigeonhole.

2. **Type "B" Personality:** This type "B" personality judge is a compassionate, warmhearted individual that can come across as kindly, down to earth, and unsophisticated. This judge intentionally appears in this manner and allows for rambling stories. This judge will listen to every detail and wants both parents to have the chance to tell everything they want heard. The danger of this personality type is, if you become too wordy, you can dig yourself into a deep hole and find yourself in the wrong pigeonhole. If you talk too much, you may give information that leads to opening a "can of worms."

## KEEP IN SYNC

A judge will only deviate from his/her established solutions when the circumstances of the case are extraordinary and unique. Once a judge makes a final decision on a case, he/she moves on to the next case, leaving you with a judicial order that is not going to be turned around easily. Keep in "sync" with your judge.

### Don't Try Waltzing
### With A Judge
### Who Is Two-Stepping

High performing sales people know their customers and tailor their "pitch" according to the personality of their client. You must do the same thing with your judge. It is critical for you to not fight the judge, but work with him/her. An individual judge is predictable. This "predictability factor" is intentional and helps to settle cases. You will learn how your particular judge rules on the various issues from your fieldtrip and doing your homework.

While sitting in the courtroom, pay close attention to the nonverbal signals used by the judge to communicate to attorneys, staff, and litigants. Take notice of the judge's nonverbal form of communication and log it in your memory bank for use when it is your turn in the barrel. You will learn what annoys a particular judge and what pleases that same judge.

Your facial expressions should be reserved in and around the courtroom, especially when adverse information is being put forth. Facial expressions of both parents are closely scrutinized by the judge at all times. Any facial gestures you make during adverse testimony will only reinforce the testimony being given.

Many litigants visually react in disbelief during adverse testimony as a way of nonverbally telling the judge that the witness is lying. It is better to keep a poker face and use your eyes to stare through the lie than to use body language to visually rebut the inaccurate information.

To make a good impression, and present an image of being a solid citizen, you need to:

- Appear honest.

- Avoid confrontations.

- Exercise patience.

- Maintain composure.

- Be controlled.

- Show a mature attitude.

- Have reliable evidence.

- Have documented records.

- Have credible witnesses.

All the above will be weighed by the judge when making decisions about your character. A well-balanced and controlled person is what the judge wants to see.

## THE ULTIMATE DECIDER

The ultimate decision about who will win custody of your children is in the hands of your judge.

- To influence a judge's final custodial decision in your favor, you need to consider your individual judge's disposition, temperament, and mood.

- A judge must believe that your primary reason for seeking custody is for the best interest of your children. You must project the image of a person who is a positive role model for his children.

When it comes down to the final round, you want to hear the judge say the magic words...

## *CUSTODY TO FATHER*

# CHAPTER 11

# TESTIMONY

There are three sides to every story in divorce court, his hers, and the truth. A judge has the demanding responsibility of sorting through the different versions, and making court orders that are appropriate. Your testimony must be:

## *RELEVANT - ON POINT - CREDIBLE*

It is virtually impossible, timewise, to give the judge a complete history of the rights and wrongs of a relationship. You must be very careful to allocate your court time and apportion it according to:

-     Defending negative accusations.
-     Pointing out mom's deficiencies.
-     Telling your positive attributes.

To apportion time among the above three important areas, you must be well prepared. Your testimony in court must consist of information that is relevant, on point, and credible.

*RELEVANT:* Relevant means giving only the information essential to the question at hand. For instance, if you have a neglect issue, then your reporting mom's conviction for shoplifting five years ago is irrelevant.

*ON POINT:* On point means only give information that has direct impact on the subject being discussed. For instance, when the judge is concerned about a babysitting problem, then only respond to the babysitting issue.

*CREDIBLE:* Credible means testimony is believable. For instance, if you are fidgeting a lot, using weird facial expressions, or using too much body language, this can affect, add, or detract from your credibility.

There is a long-standing, generalized belief that in divorce court, there are no ethics, the parties cheat, lie, and give dishonest testimony. Position yourself away from this erroneous thinking by telling the truth even when it hurts.

# GAME PLAYING IN COURT

Studies indicate that men and women think differently, talk differently, and communicate differently. Both men and women use "WORDS," but women are more adept than men when it comes to using body language, silence, tone of voice, pauses, facial gestures, and a host of other communication techniques.

Because females have superior communication skills, they do much better in court than men. These superb communication skills can be very persuasive to a judge.

**Note:** When a woman cries in court, she brings everything to a halt, sympathy goes out to her. When she regains her composure, proceedings continue. Without saying a single word, the woman has attracted attention, made her point, and taken control.

Courtrooms provide the perfect setting for game playing by both parents and their respective attorneys. The extent of any maneuvering can make it very difficult for a judge to filter through the stories and come up with the truth. It is common for a judge to receive inaccurate or misleading information. Try very hard to appear honest and separate yourself from the game players.

Your goal, when testifying in court, is to look credible and come across to the judge as a straight forward father that only has the best interests of his children at heart.

## 1.    Be Credible - Look Credible:

Appearing honest, looking credible, and sounding truthful is very important when you are testifying in court.

Judges rely on more than just WORDS of a witness to decide the credibility of an individual. Whether a witness is on the stand, at the council table, or in the audience, a judge is always watching out of the corner of his/her eye; over reading glasses, peripheral vision, and window reflections. A judge observes both the appearance and nonverbal behavior of a witness as a measure of evaluating truthfulness.

Set aside the time needed to practice your delivery in front of a mirror, with a friend, or by using a video camera. Pay close attention to any of your facial habits or body language that might be perceived as an indication of truthfulness. You are expected to be nervous, but some gestures should be avoided as they are very often considered as indicators of untruthfulness and lying:

-    Shifty eyes.

-    Irregular breathing pattern.

-    Hand wringing.

-    Facial contortions.

-    Unusual behavior.

**2.**     **Nonverbal Behavior:**

Studies conducted in courtrooms across the country have proven that the appearance and nonverbal behavior of a witness have a greater impact on judges than testimony given orally. Never under estimate the importance of your:

APPEARANCE

&

NONVERBAL BEHAVIOR

The judge is constantly watching:

- Interaction between attorney and client.

- Behavior and mannerisms between the parents.

- Reactions of the non-testifying parent.

- Facial gestures.

- Body language.

- Nonverbal expressions.

Inappropriate body language can be used as an indicator of untruthfulness. Remain calm, controlled, and stoic when you are listening to inflammatory remarks or needling insults by mom.

Your attitude and behavior should be

## Above The Fray
## not
## Chomping At The Bit

When you hear a witness lie in court, it is okay to visually show annoyance, but do not disrupt the court proceedings. You can let the judge know that you are upset in a non-threatening, and respectful manner, with a minor gesture or facial expression such as:

- A slight shake of the head.
- A rolling of the eyes.
- A shrug of the shoulders.
- A minor grimace.

Dramatically over-responding to adverse testimony, will result in your coming across to the judge as a personality that is:

## Over Reacting - Over Bearing - Over Controlling

Surveillance cameras are everywhere, in the parking lots, hallways, and courtrooms. Any odd behavior, disturbances, loud voices, in and around the courthouse will be monitored and will be detrimental to the participants. Security is very tight in family law courts due to frequent acts of violence that occur because of the highly emotional state of litigants. Innocent actions or conduct, even if well intended, will be misinterpreted by security personnel.

**Example:** Bringing roses to the divorce trial could be a well-intended, innocent act, but will immediately put the courthouse security personnel on "red alert" and you will be monitored very closely.

You do not want to stand out or draw attention to yourself by security personnel. You want to be a member of the crowd and almost invisible. Dress conservatively, look presentable, conduct yourself properly, and obey the rules.

## TESTIMONY IN COURT

Testimony comes from words expressed by litigants and witnesses, under oath, and is accepted as "truthful" until proven otherwise. The judge presumes that testimony is true, but weighs the value, importance, and relevancy of evidence presented. A judge will also be influenced by the nonverbal communication of a witness.

There is a predetermined sequence used by a court of law to hear all of the facts of the case, and in a way that is fair to both sides. This testimony sequence has been developed and modified over hundreds of years in an attempt to keep court hearings fair and efficient. The sequence and manner in which testimony is presented is how a person gets the facts before a judge without opinions from others that are unproven, self-serving, and fall within the *Hearsay Rule.* The hearsay rule excludes out of court statements which are used to offer the proof of the matter. Judges want eye witness testimony and not second hand versions of statements.

# TYPES OF TESTIMONY

## 1.  Direct Testimony:

Direct testimony is when a witness first takes the stand and is questioned by ones own attorney. The witness is asked open-ended questions and is expected to give narrative answers. For instance, a question will be phrased as follows:

*"Tell the court about your . . . ?"*

or

*"Can you please explain why . . . ?"*

The judge only wants to hear a short synopsis from you without prompting and help from your attorney. You know the questions your attorney will ask, which means you can practice ahead of time so that important facts are not left out.

Write out answers to specific questions you know will be asked by your attorney, memorize them, and practice your delivery in front of a mirror or with friends. This practice and rehearsal of your speech will result in your giving a crisp, clean, complete delivery. This speech should include all relevant and important factual information.

**Note:** Do not try to answer more than what is asked. You will have a later opportunity to give further information.

## 2.    Cross-Examination Testimony:

Cross-examination is when the opposing attorney asks you questions based on your direct testimony in an attempt to discredit you. Questions are loaded, traps are set, and confusion is intended. The purpose of cross-examination is to discount and undermine a witnesses' direct testimony.

During cross-examination, the questions asked of a witness usually call for either a YES or NO answer. The opposing attorney phrases facts within the questions allowing him/her to give a slanted presentation of those facts, such as:

*"Isn't it a fact you . . . ?"*

or

*"Isn't it true that . . . ?"*

The way to handle all questions under cross-examination is to pause briefly, and give a response that answers the question in the best light possible. An attorney is trained to put "qualifiers" into questions asked during the cross-examination that can turn everything upside down. Judges are aware of this tactic and will take this into consideration. Answers that are a problem for you can be straightened out on redirect testimony.

**Note:** All questions asked during cross-examination are strictly limited to the areas brought up in direct testimony. Any new areas must be brought up at a later time.

## 3.     Redirect Testimony:

Redirect testimony is when the witness explains answers given that were unclear because of the YES or NO answer restriction on cross-examination. Cross-examination of litigants or witnesses is intended to be argumentative, attacking and feisty. Judges expect it. Redirect testimony is a judgment call and will be made by you and your attorney, depending on time considerations.

> **Note:** You and your attorney must decide if your limited time in court should be spent rebutting on redirect, or if your limited court time should be spent on presenting new evidence.

## 4.     Relevant Testimony:

One of the bigger problem areas, for litigants in court, is wasting a judge's time on irrelevant information. It doesn't help in the decision process. A judge only wants to hear information that will shed light on the facts of the case. Judges do not have time to hear the story of your life. Only give the judge those pertinent facts that will be of assistance in making the right decisions. Do not waste the court's time by bringing up past grudges, ancient mistakes, or facts that are inconsequential. Grinding on old insults will be interpreted as an intention to hurt or anger, not to enlighten the judge.

Testimony that appears to be motivated by spite, attempt to humiliate, or embarrass, will be perceived by the judge as an immature person incapable of being a good role model. Judges will not allow parents to waste the court's valuable time to "even old scores" or indulge in "mud slinging."

Relevant testimony in a court custody battle is restricted to recent happenings, not long-past occurrences. The judge wants to hear current information that is relevant to the present situation to help him/her make a decision. Judges are not working with perfect human beings, therefore the judge must select between two imperfect parents.

A judge will exclude any testimony that may be confusing, time-consuming, or misleading. Facts that have no bearing on the issues before the court aren't allowed because of time limitations. There are other parents waiting their turn. Prepare your oral testimony in a brief, compact package of organized thoughts. Your oral testimony should consist of the issues you know will be addressed during mom's testimony. There will be no surprises in the courtroom if you have done your homework and prepared properly.

## ADMISSIBLE/INADMISSIBLE EVIDENCE

There are no juries in the family law courts, therefore, judges hear all evidence offered from both parties, admissible and inadmissible. The judge will then make the discretionary call about what evidence will be allowed in court, and what evidence will not be allowed in court. Judges are highly trained and very experienced in making the determination as to the admissibility of evidence.

You must accept all judicial decisions made by the judge and learn to work with him/her. It might be easier to understand what could be considered as "admissible evidence" if you look at a jury situation.

When there is a jury, the judge hears all evidence offered by both sides and then makes the determination as to admissibility or inadmissibility of this evidence. The admissible evidence is then presented to the jury. This two-step process ensures that the jury does not hear any evidence declared inadmissible, and therefore, prejudicial.

The jury scenario is a two-step process:

**First:**          Judges hear evidence that is damaging.

**Second:**          Judges makes a ruling as to admissibility before the jury hears the evidence.

Family law judges hearing admissible and inadmissible testimony are suppose to ignore all evidence that is considered to be inadmissible. However, hearing the prejudicial information can have a profound impact on the judge.

**Example:** When testimony has been given that mom was convicted of shoplifting ten years ago, the judge rules this as inadmissible evidence because the incident occurred a long time ago. However, the testimony will still leave an imprint of a dishonest person on the judge.

As a lay person, you're not expected to understand the legal technicalities of admissible and inadmissible evidence, so tell the judge everything you think might be helpful. The judge will then make the decision about what testimony will be admissible. When you are testifying, give short sentences and let the judge decide if more detail would be helpful.

Here are a few common scenarios and the customary judge reaction.

Dad says:          "Mom stole ten years ago."
Judge answers:     "Too remote."

------------------------------------------------------------------------

Mom Says:          "Dad was using drugs seven years ago."
Judge answers:     "Too remote."

------------------------------------------------------------------------

Dad Says:          "Mom had an affair."
Judge answers:     "Inadmissible"

------------------------------------------------------------------------

Dad Says:          "Mom was using methamphetamine a lot
                   last year."
Judge answers:     "Admissible, tell me more."

------------------------------------------------------------------------

List the historical events that have occurred during your relationship with mom that will be influential on the judge. Make your list on a small note card and keep it with you at all times to help jog your memory about the events. This list should include details that will shed light on your admirable qualities and excellent parenting skills. The list should also include the problems with mom that show her lack of good parenting skills.

## 1.    Written Documents:

Before any *written documents* can be presented in court for a judge to view, you must overcome a few hurdles:

- Authenticity of any documents must be established before it can be entered into the record.

- Writing must accurately reflect information being given.

- Personal knowledge of the writing is required.

Diaries, calendars, personal notes, school records, medical records, doctor letters, police reports, along with other writings, can be valuable to the judge for correctly understanding the real family situation. These documents can then be used as an aid for the judge to make appropriate orders. There is always an inherent danger with written documents as they can be created or altered quite easily. A judge might allow these written documents into evidence, but only after precautions have been taken as to the authenticity, accuracy, and relevance.

Photographs are also hearsay documents. The person who took the pictures is the one that needs to be in court to testify as to their authenticity. This person will be asked to testify under oath about when the pictures were taken, and whether or not they accurately depict the conditions photographed. Therefore, it is best if you take the pictures yourself.

Keep a record of all major events with the children in a diary. The more specific the better:

- Teacher/parent conferences.
- Doctor appointments.
- School functions.
- Children's activities.
- Telephonic contacts.
- Altercations with mom.

Log the information in an 8-1/2" X 11" day-timer type calendar as your diary will be considered a very reliable source. If you have your events chronicled in loose, disorganized notations, or you are fumbling around with your paperwork, the judge might assume your information is in error. Appearing disorganized and unprepared may reflect on the perceived accuracy of your records.

The judge might not read completely through your diary, however, he/she will allow you to refer to it when answering questions to give accurate dates, times, and locations of events. You can also refer to the diary for pertinent notations you put down about events that have taken place.

**Note:** A judge only allows you to use the diary when testifying as a way for you to "refresh your recollection."

Just prior to your court date, review the diary carefully so that events will be fresh in your mind. This will help you to readily flip to the appropriate sections when testifying. The review will also help you to remember events that have significance and help put matters into perspective, resulting in clarity of your testimony.

## 2. Hearsay Rule:

The legal term, *Hearsay* is extremely complex and very technical. Hearsay refers to out of court statements made to prove the truth of the matter.

Hearsay is inherently suspicious, because a witness could simply give false statements when testifying. Hearsay evidence is allowed into the court record under specific conditions when the judge thinks the evidence will be essential to the case. The judge must then weigh the value of this hearsay evidence. The hearsay rule is a hyper-complicated area of the law and you should not be too concerned with such legal technicalities. Rather, present all the evidence you consider important, and trust in the judge's legal knowledge and wisdom.

## 3. Character Witnesses:

Each parent will ask persons to testify on their behalf, and these witnesses are called, *character witnesses.* These witnesses are relatives, friends, clergymen, business associates, and other people who will give favorable testimony. Obviously, the parents only call upon those witnesses that will be validating their good character.

The judge is aware that the character witnesses brought to court by mom are going to speak highly of her and that she will not be bringing any adverse witnesses. Such witnesses can be very time consuming to the court and cumulative. Therefore, most judges will not allow excessive character witness testimony.

**4.    Impeachment Witnesses:**

An *impeachment witness* is different from a character witness. An impeachment witness is someone brought into court in an attempt to show that you are a liar.

Impeachment witnesses are used to rebut direct testimony. For instance, if you testify that you always cooked dinner, then mom can bring in her sister to testify that she was in your home every weekend and never saw you cook. he point made by the impeachment witness is not your cooking, but whether you are telling the truth. If you were lying or exaggerating about cooking meals, you probably lied about other issues as well such as: Teacher conferences, doctor appointments and other parenting activities.

**5.    Credible Witnesses:**

A *credibile witness* is not determined by ones profession or status in life, but rather by ones' perception of believability and truthfulness as seen by the judge. A recent study requested divorce judges to list the person they found to be the most believable from the following list:

1.    Police officer.
2.    Clergyman.
3.    Elected official.
4.    14 year old teenager.

Think to yourself for a moment and answer as you believe a judge would. The answer given by a majority of judges is going to surprise you. If you guessed number four, then you are right.

Analyzing the answer to the question above, you should conclude that family law judges believe teenagers are truthful. Thus, you may want to reconsider your witnesses. Judges believe teenagers have not yet learned to exaggerate or omit things on purpose when telling a story. Consequently, do not be afraid to bring a teenager into court to testify on your behalf as either:

### A Character Witness

or

### An Impeachment Witness

In family law courts, the witnesses for both parents are emotionally involved and may have axes to grind. Family feuding puts all judges in the most difficult position of dealing with good people acting at their worst.

A judge looks out each day at his/her courtroom and the scene resembles a wedding chapel with dad's people grouped together and mom's people doing likewise. Everyone in dad's group will say good things about him and bad things about mom, and mom's group will do visa-versa. A judge wants to hear factual information and not negative impressions. Judges are constantly hearing cases where:

All witnesses are *Correct* to a degree.

yet

All witnesses are *Incorrect* to a degree.

## A JUDGES' "LIE" QUESTION

By now, you should begin to appreciate the difficulty a judge has in sorting out misrepresentations, misstatements, and omissions made by the witnesses in seeking the truth. Because of constant distortions, exaggerations, deceit, fraud and lies that are encountered in the family law courts, judges have to resort to trick questions designed to find out who is lying.

The judge will use a lie question to trap a witness in a falsehood. A judge will ask a naive question intended to elicit an answer that is untrue. The reason a judge uses a lie question with a witness is to find out whether or not that witnesses testimony is to be believed at all. Oftentimes, this lie question is buried within a rapid series of quick, easy questions.

## WHEN TESTIFYING - BE TRUTHFUL

It would be devastating if you told just one teeny, tiny, little white lie, and this one small lie made the difference between winning and losing custody of your children.

## CHAPTER 12

# MASTERING THE SKILLS
# OF TESTIFYING

Your goal in court is to look truthful, project honesty and convince the judge that you would be the better custodial parent for your children. This requires developing good communication skills by using correct words and appropriate body language.

Keep in mind, it's often not:

## WHAT YOU SAY

**but**

## HOW YOU SAY IT

The language of a speech can be very memorable, but the intonation, inflection, pauses, pitch, accent, pronunciation, voice volume, body language and overall vocal delivery are what set apart great speakers from the mediocre.

The memorable speeches of the famous: John F. Kennedy, Martin Luther King Jr., Ronald Reagan, and Bill Clinton have all been outstanding, and their speeches will be remembered into the next century because of their extraordinary delivery. These famous speakers were not born with oratorical skills, they practiced and learned.

If you do not have an occupation that requires polished speaking skills, then it is important that you rehearse your speech and practice speech drills. It would be a tragedy if you could not accurately convey your message to the judge because you lacked communication skills.

There are many speaking techniques that you can learn and practice before your day in court. Practicing and rehearsing these speaking drills will make you look a lot more:

### *CONFIDENT - CREDIBLE - TRUTHFUL*

**Note:** The courtroom is not the place for you to use slang expressions, swear words or vulgarity. Language of this sort makes you look crude and immature. Your parenting skills will be measured by every facet of your personality. So you must constantly be on your toes.

# TRUTHFULNESS

Being truthful and looking truthful are not necessarily the same thing. You can be truthful yet give ineffective testimony which appears untruthful. Here are some examples of ineffective testimony that you want to avoid:

- Hesitating before certain answers.
- Stumbling over words.
- Refusing to answer.
- Responding evasively.
- Verbal missteps.

Witnesses that appear truthful when testifying give their versions of events with specificity. Liars and exaggerators usually speak in generalities. Speaking in generalities does not necessarily mean you are being untruthful. However, you may appear to be untruthful because of nervousness, confusion, or fear. Litigants that appear untruthful, when they are actually speaking the truth, end up frustrated and upset. You must set yourself apart by adding specificity to your answers when responding to questions.

Give specific details when telling your story. It will make you and your story much more believable. Dishonest testimony cannot withstand the onslaught of specific questions that will be asked during the cross-examination phase of testimony. Creating a visual picture enhances exactness and believability.

**Example:** If you testify that you do all the cooking for the children indicating you are a nurturing parent, tell the judge where you shop for groceries, what kinds of food you prepare, which ingredients you use in the salad, and other specifics.

## PROJECT HONESTY

Honesty is manifested through words, actions, and body language. People have perceptions about certain mannerisms that indicate dishonesty. Nervous habits are often interpreted as indicators of dishonesty. Pay attention to your mannerisms and habits and avoid any traits which the judge might perceive as signs of nervousness caused by being dishonest.

**Note:** Honest witnesses can appear dishonest when they: Grind teeth, flail arms, stuttering, no eye contact, and do other things which can be interpreted wrongly.

Eye movement is commonly used as a means to gauge a persons honesty. A person with shifty eyes may very well be telling the truth, however, a judge might interpret this shifty eye movement as an indicator of untruthfulness. Be conscious of your eye movement at all times in the courtroom.

When answering questions, look at the inquiring attorney directly. Keep good eye contact with the attorney and occasionally turn to the judge for effect. Get good eye contact with the judge and hold it. Always respond to questions in a firm voice. When mom is testifying, your eye contact should be on her, in a way that is non-threatening, and periodically look at the judge.

Professional actors have mastered the art of telling a story with make believe scripts, yet, the audience gets caught up in the story and actually believes the actor. Effective communication skills can be learned from numerous books available in a library.

# LINGUISTIC TECHNIQUES

Linguistic techniques are skills that can be learned from watching television, movies and reading books. We all watch courtroom dramas on television and at the movies, where actors walk into court with a problem and leave with a solution. This oversimplified attempt to solve problems in two hours or less, is not the real world, as it takes multiple court appearances to move forward in litigation. The proper uses of language (words) with strong body emphasis, results in dramatic testimony.

It is essential for you to take a fieldtrip to your local courthouse and watch an actual family law hearing in session. You will see how the proper use of linguistics supports and enhances the impact of the testimony. The best way to learn linguistic techniques used in a courtroom is by actual example. Observe how some attorneys and litigants are much more effective with the use of words and body language. Notice how a simple maneuver can have great impact.

**Note:** An attorney asking a question with intense eye contact, places great importance on an answer. However, an attorney leaning back in chair, cleaning his glasses while questioning, demonstrates the answer is less important.

When you go on your fieldtrip to the courtroom, take a notepad with you. While you listen to the drama unfold, jot down notes on linguistic techniques used by the attorneys and litigants. Then, practice the techniques learned in your car, on the way to work, in front of a mirror, or with friends. Linguistic techniques will help you get your points across more effectively, and enhance your credibility. This, in turn, will help you achieve your ultimate goal of winning custody.

## 1.    Choice Of Words:

The choice of words used when testifying in court are extremely important. Using similar words can result in completely different interpretations. Saying, *"our"* children, has the effect of a co-parent talking, whereas saying, *"my"* children, the effect is a selfish interpretation. The word *"our"* when referring to children, comes across as an acknowledgment of shared parenting responsibilities. Choice of pronouns reflects upon your attitude about parenting obligations.

The most common spoken-word in the English language is the word *"I."* Use the word, *"I"* sparingly, and only when absolutely necessary. Train yourself to think before starting a sentence with the word *"I"* as overusing the word *"I"* comes across as egocentric, boastful, and selfish. The words *"my"* and *"I"* are needed at times, but keep the usage to a bare minimum. Try to avoid using the words, *"she," "mom's name,"* or *"this woman"* particularly at the beginning of a sentence. Starting with these pronoun words comes across as accusatory. Starting in such a manner sets up a blaming situation.

*"She said . . . "*

*"**Carol** told me . . ."*

*"**This woman** lied about . . . "*

There are going to be moments when the sentence must start with the word, *"she,"* or with *"**mom's name**,"* and this can be interpreted as an attempt to shift blame and also be accusatory in nature. As often as possible, avoid using the above. This will take practice, but will be worth the effort.

## 2.    Body Language:

A judge will rely on more than words in determining the credibility of the witness. Body language is a good indicator of one's mental attitude. Some obvious examples are: A witness pointing a finger, pounding on the table, glaring at the opposition, creating disturbance, and other irritating behavior.

> **Note:** A composed witness who suddenly becomes rattled, is telegraphing there is a problem. Behavioral changes can be interpreted as an indication of lying.

While you are sitting at the council table during mom's testimony; sit upright, chest out, stomach in, and no slouching. Maintain eye contact, and periodically look at the judge when making any profound and critical points. Keep composed when adverse testimony is being given. Look confident at all times, even if you are a nervous wreck inside. Nervous body language might be regarded as the manifestations of a liar. You don't want to let nervousness be a factor in judicial decisions.

When mom is testifying and you are at the council table, keep your body movements controlled, and respectfully observe court proceedings. Minimize facial gestures, take brief notes, be very attentive, and look the judge in the eye when he/she looks at you. Your body language when hearing inflammatory testimony is going to be scrutinized very carefully by the judge. Your reactions may lock in whether the judge believes the testimony being given. Many judges are more interested in the response of a parent sitting at the council table than of the witness testifying.

## 3.    Tone Of Voice:

The tone of your voice should stay on an even level so that variations from this baseline tone can be used for effect and to give a message. Changes in your vocal pitch will be heard by the judge and can give new meaning because of the altered sound of your voice.

**Example:** Take a song recorded by various recording artists, and listen to the different renditions and styles. Listen how each version of the song is interpreted totally differently. This phonetical variation can add a totally new meaning to the same set of words.

A high-pitched voice from a male might be considered a sign of nervousness, fear, or untruthfulness. Conversely, a male with a deep, low-pitched, resonant timbre to his voice could land him a high salaried newscaster job. This low-pitched sound of voice from a male projects truthfulness and believability. Watch the newscasters on television and try to mimic their tone of voice. Use a tape recorder to record your voice so you can hear how your voice sounds to others. Then, make adjustments accordingly.

A cocky tone of voice, a mocking tone of voice, a sharp tone of voice, a sarcastic tone of voice, a negative tone of voice, all reflect poorly on the character of persons testifying. An angry tone of voice suggests the possibility of a violent temper. No judge is going to take the chance of placing children with someone who will lose control of their temper, and possibly hurt a child because of a temper tantrum. Listen to your tone of voice on a tape recorder, it will be very helpful.

**Note:** Humor does have a place in a courtroom setting, particularly when the judge is making a joke. However, a custody battle is a serious matter and humor must be displayed very cautiously. Laughing at the wrong time is childish and could be detrimental. Nervous laughter should be avoided.

**4.      2-Second Pause:**

The 2-second pause is a very effective technique to use when testifying in court. A 2-second pause is used when the person testifying takes a two-second pause before answering any questions. The purpose is to give a witness time to think, two seconds, before answering hard questions. Answering rapidly to some questions, and then pausing on others is inconsistent and could be interpreted as lying. Using this 2-second pause technique means all your answers will be given in exactly the same manner, both easy and hard. This technique adds credibility to testimony given. Police officers are trained to use this technique when called upon to testify in court. Pause for two seconds before you answer any questions, starting with the universal first question, *"state your name for the record, and spell it."*

Using the 2-second pause establishes a rhythm in your speech pattern which gives you an edge when confronted by an aggressive attorney on cross-examination. Maintaining a constant rhythm pattern in your speech will add to your believability. Uneven patterns in pausing between answers and questions, might suggest a person is taking the extra time to fabricate a story. Pause two seconds even when the answer is a simple YES or NO.

## 5.     The Long Pause:

Once you have established a rhythm with the 2-second pause, you can learn to use the extra long pause for effect. This will help you to counter an intimidating, aggressive, overbearing, attorney. Pausing on answers, shifts control over to the witness, leaving the attorney waiting for an answer. The long pause breaks the rhythm of an argumentative line of questioning.

The long pause is also very effective when faced with an emotional question. The extended pause gives you time to gain your composure, and can truly have a positive and dramatic effect when properly used. Yet can be annoying and distracting when over used.

Use the long pause when being cross-examined by an argumentative attorney who is conducting a rapid series of hostile questions. Your main reason for using this long pause is to make it more difficult for the attorney to trip you up or back you into a corner. Argumentative demeanor is difficult to counter because the attorney will be asking questions that call for a yes or no answer, leading to a trap.

You can see the trap coming when you hear the questions take on the following pattern:

*"Isn't it true that you . . ."*

*"And, isn't it also true that . . . "*

*"Isn't it a fact that . . ."*

All of the above are leading questions intended to set you up for a fall. The way to handle yourself in this situation is to slow the pace by taking long pauses before answering questions. This will break down the attorney's rhythm. Do not be antagonistic or give sarcastic answers, as the judge will see this behavior as your way of dodging difficult questions.

A judge knows when an attorney is attempting to back you into a corner, and this is considered acceptable gamesmanship by the attorney. Your using the long pause will give you the extra time necessary to answer any difficult questions. This counter-gamesmanship maneuver is acceptable.

**6.      Voice Inflection:**

The inflection you place on each word, with your voice, changes the meaning of a phrase. Placing emphasis on one word, will give one meaning, and placing emphasis on another word in the same sentence, will give it a totally different meaning. The technique is simple, yet can have a dramatic effect.

The following drill is designed to teach you this simple tactic.

Say the following phrase out loud.

*I did not say my wife is a slut to our child*ren.

Repeat the phrase out loud again.

*I did not say my wife is a slut to our children.*

We are now going to change the meaning of the phrase by having you place inflection on different words in the sentence.

Now, repeat the phrase out loud with emphasis on the word highlighted.

## *"I"*

*I, did not say my wife is a slut to our children.*

By placing emphasis on the word, *"I,"* it is implied that the speaker did not say the derogatory statement, but maybe someone else might have said it.

## *"did not"*

*I **did not**, say my wife is a slut to our children.*

By placing the emphasis on the words *"did not,"* it is implied that the speaker definitely did not make the statement, and therefore, a strong and truthful response.

## *"say"*

*I did not **say**, my wife is a slut to our children.*

By placing emphasis on the word *"say,"* it is implied that the speaker did not speak the derogatory statement, but the speaker might have written or otherwise communicated the slur.

### *"my wife"*

*I did not say **my wife**, is a slut to our children.*

By placing the emphasis on the words *"my wife,"* it is implied that the speaker may have made the remark, but directed it at someone other than his wife.

### *"slut"*

*I did not say my wife is a **slut**, to our children.*

By placing the emphasis on the word *"slut,"* it is implied that the speaker made a slur, but might have used a different word to give the insult.

### *"our children"*

*I did not say my wife is a slut to, **our children**.*

By placing the emphasis on the words *"our children,"* it is implied that the speaker made the remark to someone other than the children.

You now understand the importance of placing emphasis on an individual word or words in a sentence, and how this can change the entire meaning of the statement. The art of intonation is a skill perfected by many accomplished speakers and actors, and is considered acceptable gamesmanship. Learn this technique by watching TV talk shows, and then practice them.

## 7.    Stop When Ahead:

A fundamental tactic in a courtroom, is to stop after you have made your point with the judge, and then move on to another topic. Continuing to push on the same issue after the judge has acknowledged he/she understands your position, will only irritate him/her, and waste time. Therefore, once you have made your point with a judge, STOP, and go on to another subject. This is especially important if you have made a positive point with the judge, because annoying him/her by badgering on a specific issue, the point might get diluted or maybe even washed out.

Court hearings always involve multiple issues, and you must keep alert about when your judge gets your point so you can go on to another topic. A judge considers all issues, on both sides, before making orders, and does not have the time nor the patience to keep listening to only one issue.

You will notice from watching other cases on your fieldtrip that judges listen to both sides before making any final decisions. Observe the judge's nonverbal signals to the attorneys or litigants. A smart litigant, or attorney will stop when they think the judge understands their position. Listed here are the nonverbal signals to look for with the judge:

- Eye-contact.
- Nodding of the head.
- Facial gestures.
- Hand movements.

All of the above suggests to the judge, your point has been made and received. After receiving a nonverbal message from the judge, move on to another point and use the same technique.

## 8. Open-Ended Speech:

Prepare a brief speech for each point you want the judge to consider. During your direct testimony, you will have a chance to give a short monologue in response to an open-ended question. Your monologue must be clear, concise, and to the point.

To give an effective and compelling open-ended speech, each point should be written down on a separate index card so they can be easily referred to. Using individual index cards will help you to better organize your thoughts so important facts are not forgotten. Practice your delivery, and then make the changes needed to better your speech.

When giving your speech to the judge, turn to him/her, get eye contact, lower your voice, and then deliver your rehearsed short speech. Continue your speech until you sense the judge has heard enough. Be careful not to overuse this technique, as it loses its effectiveness if overdone. Looking the judge in the eye, and lowering your voice will project strength of conviction to your testimony.

Eye contact with the judge and the lowering of your voice is a technique that is incredibly effective when executed at the right time. Try using this technique in a conversation with friends, where suddenly you turn to one person in the group, get strong eye contact with this person before talking, lower your voice, and then make your statement. Practicing this technique on a friend will confirm the tremendous impact it makes.

**Note:** To be the most effective when making a point to a judge, turn to him/her, get eye contact, lower your voice to a deeper tone, and then deliver your speech.

## ANTICIPATE PROBLEMS

Court hearings have time limitations because the number of litigants far exceeds the number of judges available. Testimony given in court also has time constraints and, therefore, needs to be concise. Managing your time in court is a key strategic decision, as you must choose between talking about:

### The Pots And Pans
### or
### The Children

You will not have the time in court to tell the story of your life. By the time your day in court arrives, you should be well prepared to give your speech and anticipate the issues mom will be bringing up. You are going to be asked difficult questions intended to reflect adversely on your parenting skills. You must be ready to give good responses to any adverse testimony from mom or her witnesses. Since you are aware of the problem issues and have anticipated them, memorize short, punchy rebuttals.

Whenever politicians respond to questions asked by an antagonistic reporter, they usually have prepared and rehearsed short replies that cannot be edited out of context. These are called "sound bytes." You too can develop short sound bytes for difficult questions you know will be asked. Anticipation of the problem areas allows you to rehearse responses that will blunt questions.

**Note:** The question is, *"when was the last time you did drugs?"* The answer is, *"I haven't done drugs for years, have completed a 12-step program, and teach Sunday school."*

## DRAMA AWARD PERFORMANCES

Linguists confirm males and females come from totally separate cultures, live in parallel universes, and communicate in radically different ways.

**Example:** Little girls give tea parties and "chitchat," while little boys are out "playing with frogs." Little girls are developing language skills while little boys are developing physical skills.

The gender difference of males and females is ingrained at a very early age. Females interact with other females from the time they learn to speak, whereas males first interact with females at around the age of thirteen. This concept about females relating much better than males makes sense. Females engage in more intimate conversations with their peers, while males are more private, talk less, and keep things to themselves. This refinement of communication skills gives females a head start on learning to communicate from the best of the best - other females.

Women's intuition is not a myth. The female brain is developed to a much higher degree than the male brain, in areas of language, perception, and feelings. Female traits of patience, sympathy, tolerance, and compassion are the traits that make for great moms, but they are also the traits that make females great litigants. In a court hearing, where words are the weapons used by both sides, the side using extra spin on words, generally the female, is going to have an advantage. Accept the fact that females have developed a higher level of communication skills by using various techniques to get their points across.

A female is a formidable opponent in a courtroom setting because of her advanced communication skills and techniques.

- Crying on demand.
- Telegraph by facial expressions.
- Communicate with their eyes.
- Expert body language.
- Hand gestures.
- Melodramatic.
- Innuendo.

Females are all accomplished actresses, drama queens, and capable of drama award performances. In a courtroom setting, the reserved male demeanor can be easily overwhelmed visually by female histrionics.

**Note:** At a critical point of testimony, a listening female will lean forward, head erect, with intense body language. She follows the testimony with this demeanor, then jerks and slouches, communicating to the judge that important information is now being given incorrectly.

Males have traditionally relied on words alone when they are communicating. Most males do not utilize the communicating techniques of facial gestures, body position, eye contact hand gestures and body stillness that females have developed from a very young age. Make a point of watching females conversing with one another, and see if you can interpret their mindset from the body language used.

Practice Reading Female Body Language

# ENGAGING THE ENEMY

Females have genetic traits developed from being the weaker sex, and they have had to rely on deception, trickery, and cunning to counter the male strength factor. Many fathers have been out-maneuvered due to the sharper communication skills of "the enemy."

Some tactics used by mom are as follows:

1.    Mom wants a second chance, when actually she needs time to regroup from a losing position.

2.    Mom baits dad into an altercation and then uses this altercation to have dad thrown in jail. This tactic gets an immediate restraining order against dad and wins mom custody.

3.    Mom brainwashes children and then the incorrect information is repeated to a therapist.

4.    Mom files a false molestation charge against dad and uses this factor to deny dad contact with the children.

5.    Mom conceals assets, works for cash, and then wants money from dad for herself that should go to the children.

6.    Mom will craftily hit dad's hot buttons and then demand dad be psychologically evaluated.

Judges believe that when mom makes an accusation of domestic violence against dad, it is not always intended to hurt him, but that it comes from a need to regain control of a situation. If an accusation of domestic violence is made by mom against you, don't waste your court time explaining why mom is not in any danger, instead, take your girlfriend to court. This tactic will give the message to the judge that you have moved on in your life and you are not a physical threat to mom. Presence of your girlfriend in the courtroom will:

- Counter the innuendo of a "broken hearted nut case," that wants mom back.

- Rattle mom, keep her off balance, and throw her off her gameplan.

Potential for serious violence is extremely high in the family law courtroom. Family law judges get very concerned about situations when mom alleges that dad wants her back. The jilted male syndrome is when murders occur. Studies of stalkers find that 25% of cases end in physical violence, 2% in murder.

A jealous, possessive male will be perceived as a control freak and maybe a precursor to violence. Females take advantage of this concern over domestic violence, and use words and body language to convey a false fear in an attempt to put the judge and bailiff on red alert. Any male that comes across as a control freak to the judge, is going to be in a difficult position. A controlling personality is considered the most dangerous in the courthouse.

React Dispassionately To Harsh Accusations

# CHAPTER 13

# MOM'S - DIRTY TRICKS

Divorce can bring out the negative personality traits of the female mindset - deceit, spite, and greed, to name a few. You can take comfort in knowing that other fathers have been similarly pounded upon, and have prevailed in a custody battle. You can learn how to combat the dirty tricks used by mom in a vicious custody battle through the experiences of those fathers who have gone before you.

Some mothers resort to lying, cheating, stealing, forging, and other yellow-bellied tactics in an attempt to seek revenge on dad. They may not be primarily concerned with the well being of the children. The children who are caught up in the middle of this brutal warfare are the real victims.

Dirty tricks are those mean ploys meant to torment dad and to payback old grudges. The motivation is based on revenge, yet mom's dirty tricks throw dad off balance and cause him to react immaturely. The end result of this male baiting is a leg-up for the female in the court proceedings. A male taking the bait feeds into the syndrome and moves a step backwards.

Moms involved in a nasty custody battle call upon female friends for advice and female networking results in consistent patterns to the dirty tricks. Repetitious plots by mom, against dad, are seen over and over again by judges, and they expect dad to handle these dirty tricks in a rational manner. Keep in mind, it is not what you have been accused of, but how you respond and react to accusations that measures your mental strength.

**Note:** The judge will discretely watch your reaction to explosive, adverse testimony. The visual maturity level of your reaction can be more impacting to the judge than the audio reception of the witnesses words.

A father caught up in this agonizing position must learn to handle the "dirty tricks" by mom. He must realize that mom's negative tactics are intended to keep him from getting custody of the children. These cowardly maneuvers by mom are only meant for revenge. The counter-maneuvers for a dad, when confronted with dirty tricks by mom, is to use what has worked for other fathers faced with similar situations. Trust in the knowledge that for every mom dirty trick, there is a successful dad counter-maneuver.

## DIRTY TRICKS - COUNTER-MANEUVERS

When mom resorts to underhanded methods of combat in a custody battle, dad must blunt this fighting by implementing a correct counter-maneuver. We have listed the most common dirty tricks used by moms so you can:

- Anticipate them.
- Watch them develop.
- Head them off.
- React appropriately.

Dirty tricks used by moms in family law courts have all been used before. Stick with the correct counter-maneuvers and do not try to reinvent the wheel. Moms stooping to the level of using dirty tricks are operating with devious and spiteful agendas. Dad must let the judge know mom's true motives without making himself appear as an equally culpable participant in the payback.

**Note:** Fathers trying to fend off mom's dirty tricks through "tit for tat" methods will lose ground because of gender bias. It is acceptable for females to act out in court, but not for males.

Moms that set off false alarms against dad, do it to gain an advantage. The false smokescreens are used in the hopes that a judge will take a conservative approach, "better safe than sorry" and give custody to mom. When mom makes false allegations, it forces dad to waste time, energy, and money defending charges. Mom's true intention is to box out dad.

The most common dirty tricks are repetitious and come up in court all the time. Study the counter-maneuvers outlined that are relevant to your situation.

**1.** **MOM FRUSTRATES DAD'S CONTACT:**
Mom does everything possible to keep the children from having contact with dad. Mom's purpose is to allege that dad does not have time for the children, nor does he have a close relationship with them. Each time mom thwarts dad's contact it appears she has a valid reason. Mom might allege the following:

- False illnesses and doctor appointments.
- Enrollment in extracurricular activities.
- Invitations from school friends.
- Not at home or already asleep.

Moms will conjure up some reason why the children are not available for dad. Moms real purpose is to make it impossible for dad to have contact with his children.

**DAD'S COUNTER-MANEUVER:**
Dad must keep a detailed diary and log all mom's denials of contact with the children. Keep a list of people who will come to court and testify for you. You may have to ask police for assistance to enforce your rights. Police officers respond better to polite, courteous, and sincere requests for help. Written reports of the incidents need to be filed with the police department closest to where the problem occurred. This could mean multiple filings with different police departments. Written documentation will help to convince the judge of the intentional frustration by mom. The judge will want to take measures to relieve the police departments from wasting their time on a situation that can be easily remedied by a judge.

**2.** **MOM DENIES DAD ALL CONTACT:**
Mom conceals the children from dad by not giving him her telephone number nor letting him know where she is presently living. This is not uncommon, and very often is in direct disobedience of a court order. Mom may move out of the area just to prevent dad from having contact with the children.

**DAD'S COUNTER MANEUVER:**
It is a crime for a parent to conceal children from the other parent. This can be a reason for a switch in custody. If dad thinks that mom is concealing the children, then the *Child Abduction Unit* of the District Attorney's Office should be contacted immediately for help in locating the children. Searching for children can be very expensive. Most fathers do not have the funds to finance such a search which keeps him from contact with his children.

Dad should file a missing person's report with the local police department. Getting police involved in the search accesses governmental resources that are not available to lay people. Dad should bring along with him any reliable witnesses to establish that the complaint is legitimate and not a fleeing, battered mom. This will also help to head off any later allegations of physical abuse.

If mom is presently in a shelter, and has made the charge of domestic violence, dad will not be told where children are residing. It is common for a mom to allege she is a victim of domestic violence even though there are neither police reports nor medical reports to document those accusations. Usually she will be given the benefit of the doubt. This forces dad to go back into court to learn the whereabouts of his children.

3. **MOM SAYS - "NO MONEY, NO CONTACT":**
Mom will not allow dad to see the children unless money changes hands in her direction. Mom may use the children as pawns in what becomes a profitable business venture. Extortion against dad regarding money issues, deprives children of a healthy parental relationship. Some moms increase the tension by telling children that their father is living a life of luxury while they are forced to struggle financially and to go without special items and activities.

**DAD'S COUNTER MANEUVER:**
Mom's refusal to allow dad contact with his children, is in violation of a court order if dad has *"specified"* visitation time periods with his children. If the court orders state, *"reasonable"* visitation, then this allows mom to dodge charges of refusal because of money reasons, as she can say the denials were based on her interpretation of the word reasonable. The term reasonable is vague, uncertain and subject to mom's interpretation. Reasonable visitation orders require a dad to go back into court and get specific time periods that can be enforced by a police department. Mom's refusal to comply with a "specified" visitation schedule is a contempt of court, and a criminal violation. The contempt of court must be filed in family law court and these can be hard cases to win. A contempt of court conviction is a serious matter and can result in jail time. The possibility of a jail sentence is going to get mom's attention, and is likely if she is repeatedly in violation of refusing to obey the court orders. It may take two or three convictions before mom sees the inside of a jail cell. The contempt citation is rarely granted in visitation issues.

4. **MOM BRAINWASHES CHILDREN:**
Mom tells the children wild and outrageous stories about dad. These stories frighten the children, and make them afraid to spend time with their father. Mom's motivation is revenge. Vengeful moms tell the children that dad does not care about them, blame dad for financial hardships, or wants her new husband/boyfriend to take over the role of father boxing biological dad out of the picture.

**DAD'S COUNTER-MANEUVER:**
Restraining orders can be obtained from the court to stop any disparaging or derogatory remarks by a vengeful mom. The problem lies in proving that the negative statements were made, because the children are usually the only witnesses. When mom is confronted with a brainwashing charge, she frightens the children by telling them that they will be responsible for her going to jail if they "snitch" her off.

If restraining orders are not effective and mom continues brainwashing the children, then a contempt of court action can be filed. This contempt of court action is a powerful tool to use to stop negative remarks and conduct by mom. Contempt is a very complicated legal procedure, and even attorneys have a hard time proving the case. Judges tend to lecture moms that brainwash children instead of taking more drastic measures. Often, a judge will send parents back to mediation when the basis of the contempt action involves custody or visitation.

The real irony is, when a dad disobeys child support orders he lands in jail - a mom disobeying a visitation order generally gets a lecture. Keep a log.

5. **MOM PUSHES DAD'S "HOT BUTTONS":**
Mom deliberately pushes on dads' hot buttons trying to get an irrational reaction that will make him look bad in court. When mom pushes dads' hot button, she is not interested in the problem she is quarreling over, but just wants to provoke an incident that will make dad look irrational. An inappropriate response is what mom is hoping for.

**DAD'S COUNTER MANEUVER:**
The correct response is to not engage the enemy. Mom can't win a tug-of-war if dad refuses to tug on the other end of the argument. By not responding to mom's hostile actions, dad will project maturity. Realize "tit for tat" responses will not work. Dad should just simply zip his lips, maintain his composure, and keep his body language controlled when mom is provoking him.

6. **MOM SABOTAGES COUNSELING:**
Mom attends counseling sessions and then tells friends, relatives, and the children, she is trying to cooperate with dad on the parenting problems. In actuality, mom is using her attendance in counseling as a ploy to shift the blame to dad for the family problems. This dirty trick is intended to make mom look good, and dad look bad.

**DAD'S COUNTER MANEUVER:**
An effective counselor must be fair and not take sides with either parent. A counselor appearing one-sided will only cause the other parent to stop going to the sessions. Dad needs a counselor who is neutral, but sees through mom's ploy of pretending to interact, when she is really just trying to make herself look blameless and make dad look at fault.

7.     **MOM USES SUPPORT MONEY FOR HERSELF:**
Mom uses child support money to advance her lifestyle instead of benefiting the children. Child support money is tax-free income to mom and can be used anyway she so desires. The child support money should not be used to support mom's lifestyle, partying, vacations, automobile, boyfriend, or drug habits. There are necessary expenses incurred in raising children, but there is a point when the child support money exceeds the needed expenditures for the children.

**DAD'S COUNTER MANEUVER:**
Dad should try for an agreement whereby some of the child support money will be saved for future purposes. Funds can be placed in a trust account for educational purposes. This agreement must be in writing, with both parents signatures, and then signed by the judge. It is easier to get such an agreement signed in the courthouse, when both of the attorneys are present. Also, this is the time when mom is publicly forced to show her concern for the children's future needs. Older children know if they are benefiting from all of the child support money and if mom is using child support to better her lifestyle.

Child support is based on incomes of the respective parents and any subsequent changes should be addressed in a new court action. Child support is not automatically reduced when dad's income decreases.

**Note:** Direct purchase of personal items by dad such as: Clothing, groceries, medicine, and other items cannot be offset from court ordered child support, unless a provision has been included in the court order.

**8.** **MOM NEGLECTS CHILDREN:**
Mom does a poor job of parenting, yet not serious enough to call for police intervention nor cause an investigation by social services. Some examples of marginal parenting are:

- Dirty house.
- No food in refrigerator.
- Unkempt children.
- Frequent school absences.
- Health needs neglected.

**DAD'S COUNTER MANEUVER:**
Photographs of a sloppy home, unkempt children, and dangerous conditions, are excellent evidence of neglected children. School records and letters from teachers are also helpful, as they come from unbiased sources. Testimony from neighbors about unhealthy conditions can be very persuasive.

Neglectful parenting is difficult for a judge to evaluate and, therefore, hard to prove. Serious problems should be reported to, and investigated by, the police department or *Child Protective Services (C.P.S.)*. Immediate dangers to children are handled by the police department and the children are removed from the home. Thus, family law judges are dealing with situations where neither C.P.S. nor the police have intervened. If dad thinks it is necessary to make a report to C.P.S., before making that call, he should seek advice from a responsible friend or relative that will testify on his behalf in court that the report was absolutely necessary, and not a harassment technique. If C.P.S. takes no action, the motivation for dad's call might be suspect. C.P.S. is overburdened with serious cases, and they do not have the resources for frivolous reports.

9.  **MOM COMMITS WELFARE FRAUD:**
Mom wants custody of the children only because of the welfare monies that go with the children. Some moms will commit welfare fraud by working for undeclared cash in jobs such as: Waitress, house cleaner, day care provider, or other under the table cash paying jobs.

Most welfare fraud cases involve moms failing to report other income. Dads are vigorously hounded by the District Attorney's Office to reimburse the government for any welfare funds used for their children. If moms were to be thrown in jail when they are caught committing welfare fraud, (as happens to dads for not paying child support) custody of the children would automatically go to dad. However, usually mom's only punishment for committing welfare fraud is an adjustment in her grant.

**DAD'S COUNTER MANEUVER:**
Criminal charges for welfare fraud are only filed when substantial amounts of money are involved, and there is well-documented evidence available. Welfare fraud is very difficult for the government to prove because of the cash payments with lack of records or eyewitness.

A private investigator may be required to accumulate enough evidence to convince law enforcement to file a crime report. Attempting to gather information yourself about moms' surreptitious income, is not a wise move because there is a danger that your activities might be interpreted as the crime of stalking. Private investigator fees can be well worth the investment.

10.  **MOM ABUSES CHILDREN:**
Mom abuses the children either by her active involvement or by her passively standing by while someone else abuses the children. Abuse of the children can be mental as well as physical. Oftentimes the abuse comes from a boyfriend, stepfather, or step-siblings.

**DAD'S COUNTER MANEUVER:**
Restraining orders can only restrict the two parents, not a third party. However, the judge can order a parent to keep children away from certain, named individuals. Caution is the watch word as judges want to protect children and will grant the restraining order even with very little evidence. Restraining orders can be obtained to restrict any corporal punishment of children. Mental abuse is generally in the form of improper discipline techniques and harassment. Judges will preclude such conduct by way of a restraining order.

Family law judges expect serious emergencies regarding child abuse to be handled by Child Protective Services, or police departments. Dad should take photographs to show the seriousness of the abuse because judges want to see medical evidence. If there is any doubt about the child's injuries, dad must take the child to a doctor or hospital to check out the injuries. Medical care providers are required to report suspected child abuse to appropriate government agencies. Medical providers are "mandated reporters," and their reports are taken very seriously.

**Note:** Not wanting children ending up in foster care is not a good reason for refusing to report suspected abuse. Failure to protect your children is a criminal offense.

10.   **MOM FILES FALSE CRIMINAL CHARGES:**
Mom files false criminal charges in an attempt to gain an advantage, somewhat like a "preemptive strike." Any false allegations, by mom, results in dad being harassed and hounded by governmental officials at no cost to her. The allegation itself places a cloud over dad because if he is charged with a crime, he may not be considered an adequate custodial parent. A guilty until proven innocent thinking prevails.

**DAD'S COUNTER MANEUVER:**
A false charge against dad must be dealt with very quickly. The longer a false charge goes unresolved, the longer the doubtfulness of the alleged crime, and mom has custody of the children. A family law judge will wait until after the resolution of criminal proceedings before fully addressing issues regarding children. After an acquittal or dismissal of charges, the alleged misconduct may still factor into the custody equation.

Family law judges are leery about making changes in the living arrangements of the children when they are already established in a home environment. It is imperative to quickly resolve any false criminal charges, as the judge will be confronted with a situation whereby the children have been in the custody of mom and are reluctant to uproot them from their present surroundings. Filing false criminal charges is a crime, yet hard to get the government to prosecute because of the difficulty in proving mom's wrongful intent. If mom has filed false criminal charges, dad should vigorously seek prosecution of mom for the false filing and keep pressure on the legal system to prosecute.

**12.** **MOM GETS A SPY:**
Mom gathers up adverse information on dad from mutual friends, co-workers, and relatives. Mom has tricked these people into relaying facts that she can, in turn, present in court to make dad look bad. This is usually the time when in-laws become outlaws.

**DAD'S COUNTER MANEUVER:**
Anyone can tell the same story using a different twist, leaving out important facts, changing emphasis, and create an entirely new and different story. In order to twist the events and make the new version believable, there must be a basis in true facts. Mom needs raw information that can be distorted into a falsehood. Accordingly mom needs someone to provide her information about dad which can then be inaccurately presented to the judge.

Dad must keep his personal life very private while in an ongoing custody battle. He should not discuss anything he does not want to get back to mom. Assume anything said, can and will be used against you in a court of law.

### *SILENCE IS GOLDEN*

If you know the identity of moms' spy, do not let on, as she will just get someone else. Instead, manipulate the spy by giving false leads that will cause mom to waste time and energy on wild goose chases. Misinformation and false leads, which are attempted to be used as weapons against you, will destroy moms credibility.

# GUERILLA WARFARE

Brutal, ferocious, custody brawls turn into guerilla warfare when mom uses underhanded tactics. The never ending feuding, continuous harassment, and perpetual frustration is a fate that no man or woman deserves. The early stages of a custody battle are devastating to a father.

Pearl Harbor sneak attacks where a father comes home to a vacant house, empty bank accounts, whereabouts of children unknown, and court documents left on table to read. The strategy in this situation is to remain cool, calm, and collected. Realize that you are going to lose the first few rounds, all fathers start from behind. Your objective during this initial shockwave is to survive the blast and be in good shape for the remaining rounds. Moms using this scorched earth approach, are trying to set the custody decision early in the game.

Cruel, underhanded tactics cause severe psychological damage to children. Vindictive behavior by mom makes it very hard for dad to maintain his own psychological well-being, let alone to take the appropriate attitude of turning the other cheek. Fighting fire with fire is only detrimental to the children, and your mature conduct in such a hostile environment will be looked upon with approval by the family law judge. It is vital for a father to be of sound mind when he is requesting custody of his children.

The strategy for a dad caught up in such a psychodrama, is to pull back from the fray, keep above the pettiness, conserve energy, and preserve finances. Let mom be the one to drain her resources by wearing down her support group and her finances. A counterstrike through payback tactics is not a good way for dad to respond to guerrilla tactics. The result is getting sucked into a petty feud that cannot be won.

## ROPE-A-DOPE

A father caught up in a raging custody battle should know when to pull back and take cover. After surviving the blast, he can then reassess, regroup, and rearm. When mom is in a knockout mentality, she is not open to negotiations. Dads' ability to survive the knockout is what will force mom into negotiating a settlement. Muhammad Ali very successfully defended his heavyweight championship title against the younger, stronger George Foreman by covering, blocking, conserving energy, and then knocking out fatigued Foreman. Ali called his strategy rope-a-dope.

Think of a custody battle as a 15 round prize fight, where the winner is not decided until the final round. Moms generally win the first 5 rounds of a custody battle. The traditional mom bias gives her an advantage in the early stages of litigation.

**Note:** A father's strategy during the first 5 rounds is to hang tough, avoid a knockout, remain standing, and be prepared to address the real issues.

The rope-a-dope strategy is the correct counter maneuver to guerrilla warfare in the early rounds. Responding in kind will be tempting, as the reflexive tendency to defend mom's charges by an aggressive counterattack is only natural. Dad must understand that mutual combat only feeds into her charges of immature behavior. This is the time to act restrained and polite. However, the planning and strategizing phase should begin immediately by: Compiling important data, taking photographs, keeping a diary and gathering witnesses.

A custody battle is very expensive, time consuming, and exhausting. You want to survive the experience without depleting your bank account and with your dignity in tact. A never-ending conflict has no winner and the children are the biggest losers.

## CHAPTER 14

# FAMILY DISINTEGRATION

The disintegration of the family has altered the American way of life, resulting in government intervention to solve the social problems that were once resolved within the family. Today, it is easier to divorce than it is to work at solving family problems. The result is a fatherlessness America.

The individual right of divorcing parents outweighs the negative impact fatherlessness causes on the lives of children. Children are paying the price, fatherless homes produce: 71% of teenage pregnancies, 63% of youth suicides, 90% of runaway children, 75% of children in chemical abuse centers, 71% of high-school dropouts, and 85% of incarcerated juveniles. Also, 84% of reported sexual abuse occurs in single parent homes and 64% of the perpetrators are the mom's boyfriend.

Times have changed dramatically. The typical 1990's family has evolved from the 1950's era of father/breadwinner and mother/homemaker to both parents working outside the home. Children are growing up in daycare centers and are coming home to empty houses which bring about a "latchkey" generation.

The social clock cannot be turned back to a time gone by when a father sacrificed time with the children to provide security for the family unit. In today's household, dad is preparing meals, helping with homework, transporting, doing laundry, bathing children, reading bedtime stories, extracurricular activities, and doing many other child rearing responsibilities. Contemporary fathers see themselves as equal participants in the parenting process. This new role of fatherhood should be fully recognized by family law judges and factored into the custodial decision.

Until this past generation, the family unit has been the guiding force in developing a child's character and instilling moral values. The fall of the Roman Empire has been attributed to the undermining of dignity and sanctity of the home. When the Roman family unit crumbled, so too did the Roman Empire.

The disintegration of the family unit today, is an ongoing social problem that has horrendous future ramifications for our nation's children. Families can no longer be counted on to give children a solid foundation of moral principles. There is a simple answer to this void created by easy divorce - allow fathers to stay plugged in as parents after separation. Children are being deprived of the guiding force of a father in their lives, and should not be treated as an every other weekend visitor.

Fathers Do Not Divorce Their Children!

# FATHERLESSNESS

Fatherlessness has created a nightmare that touches us all. This fatherless phenomena result in children growing up in a life of poverty. Statistics show that one out of five children is living below the federal poverty level guideline. Children are being raised by a single-parent in 22% of all homes nationwide, and in some cities this rate is over 50%.

A statement from The National Research Council says, fatherlessness in our society is the greatest family challenge of our era. Over the past 20 years attention has been on the role of women and plight of children. The missing factor is the male role model. Surveys show that 83% of all children identify father as their primary role model, and as the person most respected and relied upon for their future. This high percentage of children selecting fathers as their role model, validates the natural bonding of children to their fathers. In spite of this sociological need, too many children are still living apart from their father.

Fatherless families create major social problems, which in turn requires governmental intervention into the lives of children. The price of fatherlessness to our nation is in the billions of dollars. If government spent more money on preventive measures for children, rather than on programs after family breakups, our nation would be better served.

Fatherlessness is a direct cause to the high crime rate that indirectly affects all of us. Without a father in the home drug usage increases 17% and criminal activity is off the charts. Reducing criminal activity will make our lives safer, healthier, and more economical. We must keep fathers involved in the day to day lives of children on the criminal path.

## CHILDREN AT RISK

In the history of this nation, the level of violence inflicted on children is unprecedented. Children are at high risk of injury and death, not by disease, accident, or wild animal attacks, but in their own homes. The main perpetrators of this child abuse, are mom's boyfriend, stepfathers, and fathers. Fathers caught up in the family law system must realize that they automatically fall into the suspect category of potential abusers. The irony is that biological fathers are under the microscope of the legal system, whereas boyfriend and stepfather are outside the system. Yet, 64% of the perpetrators are the mother's boyfriend.

The national death rate from child abuse of over 2,000 children annually is the force driving the overuse of monitored contact of fathers with children . Most child fatalities are caused by raging, out of control males with children under four (4) years of age. The shaking baby syndrome accounts for about one-fourth of all deaths. The perpetrator is trying to stop the baby's crying and not intending bodily harm to the child. Monitored visitation is the standard and automatic response by judges when there is even the slightest evidence of violence. Thus, a long-ago incident of inappropriate anger maybe brought up in court by mom, judge gets concerned, and the result is monitored visitation and guilty until proven innocent.

Family law judges know of this high risk to children and the overuse of false allegations. Moms do not complain in family law court about boyfriends/stepfathers and so the judge has only one person to interrogate, biological father. The responsibility for protecting children from dangerous short-term boyfriends and abusive stepfathers is up to natural fathers.

# DAD'S WELL-BEING

A father battling for custody must prove to a judge that he is a grounded, stable, and mature individual. This can be hard to do at a time when dad's life is being turned upside down. When mom takes extreme measures to intentionally keep the pressure up, dad must not resort to using alcohol or drugs to relieve his stress. The substance abuse issue will override years of good parenting. Stress levels must be dealt with by conventional methods of relief. Consult a physician, seek out counseling, join a workshop, and read books. Keep your mind clear to predict mom's dirty tactics and be ready mentally to meet her with well-thought out counterstrokes.

The tendency to relieve anxiety through use of medication or alcohol, is not a wise move. A mind clouded with alcohol or drugs cannot function at the level necessary to win a nasty custody battle, causing him to lose due to errors in judgment of an unstable thought process.

A father accused of drugs/alcohol abuse will be asked to test, and may be required to randomly test.

- Marijuana is detectable for up to thirty (30) days.
- Methamphetamine up to three (3) days.
- Cocaine up to three (3) days.
- Alcohol up to twenty-four (24) hours.

Random testing is accomplished by giving a person notice. Then, a test must be taken within twenty-four (24) hours. Failure to test is considered a "dirty test."

Allegations of drug/alcohol abuse come up quite often during mediation, and some courts do immediate testing of both parents. A dirty test will justify future random testing, and possibly result in monitored visitation orders. Monitored visitation orders can take years to turn around. High litigation costs will be incurred before the monitored visitation is lifted.

Anyone having a record of substance abuse such as: Drunk driving, possession, sales, or a dirty test, should enroll in a twelve-step program to prove that there is no longer a problem. A person should not be punished for past indiscretions. Regular attendance in a twelve-step program will help to alleviate concerns of child endangerment. A person enrolled in a substance abuse program is seen as someone who wants to improve one's lifestyle. Keep in mind that court personnel is very conservative and will take precautionary measures whenever an allegation of substance abuse is made. A father wanting custody must show a lifestyle that is appropriate for children:

- Well-balanced meals.
- Proper sleeping arrangements.
- Regular church attendance.
- Healthy relationships.
- Support of relatives.
- Extracurricular activities.
- Stable and secure environment.

Take good care of yourself, and keep a structured, well-balanced lifestyle through: Eating well, getting plenty of sleep and taking part in physical activities. Projecting a healthy appearance in front of the judge, will show a positive person that can provide great things for his children.

# BACKUP TEAM SUPPORT

1. **FATHER SUPPORT GROUPS:**
Support groups for fathers are becoming more common and located throughout the country. The purpose of these fathers rights groups is to exchange information about mediators, judges, attorneys, and counselors in your local area and propose changes in legislation. You can also seek the advice of other fathers who have already been through the system.

Use this opportunity to verbalize your issues and get help from fathers that have experienced similar situations, however, do not let the session turn into female bashing. Participating in a father support group can improve your mental outlook and lessen the anxiety of a custody battle.

You will gain invaluable insights into your local family court system, how it works, idiosyncrasies of local court personnel, and pitfalls to be avoided. Other fathers might give solid advice and recommendations for dealing with a specific problem. Suggestions from other fathers who have gone through a custody battle, can only add to your database. Learn from their experiences. Find out the strategies, tactics and maneuvers they used, and how they fared.

**Note:** If you cannot find a local fathers rights group, get in touch with us and we will provide you with names and telephone numbers in your area.

2. **FEMALE CONFIDANTS:**
The processing of a female brain is much different from that of a male brain. A female can evaluate your situation from a female point of view, and give you an entirely different perspective of things. Be very careful in selecting a female confidant as you do not want to be betrayed.

It is much better if the female friend does not know mom, because then she will not be influenced by past history. A mutual friend might have mixed allegiances, and because of this, could end up working both sides of the fence. Be careful.

3. **ATTORNEY AND STAFF:**
Your attorney will have knowledge of your local court system, individual judges, and the mediation department. Messages can be relayed through office staff and it might not be necessary to speak directly with your attorney on each telephone call you make to the office. You must have confidence in your attorney who will be familiar with your case, frames the issues, knows the law and performs in court. Keep your attorney informed of any new and important facts, write them down, and fax or mail data to the law office so that your file is kept up to date.

When in court with your attorney, your conduct will be noted. It would be very foolish for you to display anger or frustration at your attorney. Clients acting out of control with their own attorney will be construed as unbalanced personalities.

4. **THERAPISTS AND COUNSELORS:**

Therapists and counselors are being relied upon by the court more frequently in family law cases. It is common to use counseling in those situations where parents are at odds with each other. The adversarial and confrontational atmosphere of a court of law, can rattle even the most stable of individuals. Courtrooms are not a healthy place for the American family.

Participation in counseling does not mean one has a mental disorder, it demonstrates a desire to solve ones problems with the help of a professional mental health expert. Making the decision to consult with a professional counselor, will be beneficial as it appears you are trying to work through your family problems with the assistance of an expert. You will not be penalized for attendance in counseling.

5. **CLERGY:**

Clergymembers are often asked to help families going through divorce as they are experienced in dealing with broken family situations. Clergymembers have access to many organizations that provide support to families breaking apart. Negotiations take on a less combative nature when conducted by a member of the clergy.

Religious persons can be of great help to the family during this very difficult time. If you do not attend a church regularly, ask a close friend for a recommendation. A member of the clergy makes a good character witness in court, and are always willing to come to court and testify.

## NEEDLESS CHILDHOOD ANGUISH

A child's greatest fear, at all ages, is being separated from a parent. *Separation anxiety* is experienced by all children who are living apart from one of their parents. This medical condition is to be expected in all divorces, but is unnecessary. Frequent and sufficient contact with a non-custodial parent would alleviate this condition.

**Note:** The standard visitation of every other weekend for the non-custodial parent means, a child will go (14) days without contact with a parent that the children have relied upon each day in their lives.

Children and fathers that have been abruptly disconnected from one another, are experiencing an emptiness that can only be understood by those who have gone through the experience. A child being deprived of the basic human right of sharing time with a father, undergoes psychological trauma that might never be reversed.

Needless childhood anxiety is preventable if children were allowed to share equal time with both parents. Shared parenting is especially needed for children at the beginning of the family breakup, because very often the children feel they are somehow responsible. Children that are enduring separation anxiety need to feel loved and secure. A feeling of abandonment will only cause unnecessary fright for these children. This mental condition can lead to physical disorders which then play into the courtroom drama and can affect the outcome of the case.

When children are lead to believe dad has abandoned the family, the children are being set up for psychological problems. The pain and anguish children suffer because of divorce, would be unnecessary if equal time with each parent was the rule. Children should not be without the guidance and support of a father, as this impedes their emotional development and character growth. In spite of the known damage to society, little is done to alleviate the problem of one quarter of the population under the age of (18) growing up without a father.

Children's feeling separation anxiety, can lead to medical depression which is a serious problem. It causes biological and chemical changes in the brain and nervous system. Symptoms can range from agitation, fatigue, nervousness, sleep disorders, severe depression, and suicidal thoughts. Psychological disorders need to be immediately assessed by a professional mental health expert, as depression is highly treatable and suffering can be avoided.

**Note:** The tragedy of separation anxiety in children would be better handled by the preventive measure of allowing children to be with each parent for 50% of the time.

Children need to know that they are not to blame for the breakup of their parents. This guilt syndrome is experienced by every child going through a family separation. Children love their parents equally and need to be reassured that both parents will always be there for them, no matter what. The universal dream of all children from broken families is that their parents will one day get back together.

During this difficult time of transition, a father should be as honest as he can with his children. He must give very serious thought about what the children can handle depending on their age and maturity level at the time of the family breakup. When children are included in the family discussions, they adjust much better to change.

**Note:** Judges do not take kindly to situations where the children know what is going on in court. When children know specifics about the court proceedings, the parent is held responsible by the judge.

Some children know too much about the problems of the parents when they separate, and this is a very unhealthy situation for children. Therefore parents must be careful about what they tell their children as court personnel will want to know why the children are so involved in the family problems. Parents will be criticized for using children as pawns in the custody struggle. It is in your best interest not to discuss the intimate details of the problems with the children.

Listening to children's opinions, and giving them options whenever possible, instills a feeling of involvement that will result in healthy, well-adjusted children. Many court systems will not allow children, no matter the age, to give direct input into the custody decision. This inability to have a say in their destiny, is the single most common complaint of children going through a custody battle.

# CHILDREN'S RIGHTS

- **CHILDREN** have the right to love both their parents equally without being subjected to another parent's hurt or anger.

- **CHILDREN** have the right to have a loving and meaningful relationship with each of their parents independently.

- **CHILDREN** have the right to be free from any involvement, used as either spy, messenger, or bargaining chip in their parents personal battles.

- **CHILDREN** have the right to appreciate unique differences of both sides of families, and not be caught in the middle of which side is "better" or "worse."

- **CHILDREN** have the right to be free from any questions about the other parent's private life.

- **CHILDREN** have the right to see parents treat each other in a courteous and respectful manner.

- **CHILDREN** have the right to see their friends and to continue their social activities without the fear of losing time with either parent.

- **CHILDREN** have the right to remain as children and not be treated as an adult.

# CHAPTER 15

# LEGALESE

At the conclusion of the mediation session, you may be asked to sign a written document, on preprinted forms, that have multiple pages. The preprinted forms are used for parents to list mutually agreed upon issues that will not have to be addressed in court. This written document reduces oral discussions at time of trial because the court will follow the written agreement signed by the parents. Written agreements on preprinted court forms, signed by the parents, become a court order at time of trial.

The custody/visitation issue is negotiated back and forth between attorneys and litigants until a mutual agreement is made with both parents. You will be presented with a written document that once signed by the judge, will become an order of the court. The stress of legal negotiations can overwhelm and confuse the average person.

Court forms are different in every courthouse, and are constantly undergoing changes. Listed below are some examples of paragraphs that are on most court forms. The forms have boxes to check and can be modified by crossing out portions, and making additions for items you want that are not covered. Studying the examples below will familiarize you with legal terminology, and help you to remember those things you do not want to forget. Read and mark the examples provided using the exact wording of the paragraphs when appropriate to your particular situation. Check off the paragraphs you want included in your court order, take them to court with you, and request that the exact wording be included.

Reading, familiarizing and marking the wording you want used in your court case, will prepare you ahead of time for court day. The preprinted forms are available in family law courtrooms, not the clerk's office, so go to the courthouse and get the forms. When the time comes for you to sign your name on a preprinted court document, you will be ready.

## CHILD CUSTODY/VISITATION AND RELATED ORDERS
### The Minor Children Of The Parties Are:

| NAME | BIRTH DATE | AGE |
|------|-----------|-----|
| _____ | _____ | \_\_\_\_ |
| _____ | _____ | \_\_\_\_ |
| _____ | _____ | \_\_\_\_ |
| _____ | _____ | \_\_\_\_ |

## PARTIES HEREBY STIPULATE AND AGREE TO THE ITEMS CHECKED BELOW, AND THAT COURT SHALL MAKE THE FOLLOWING ORDERS:

____ Temporary Orders pending a trial of this action or further order of court.

____ Orders For Modification.

**JOINT LEGAL CUSTODY** of the minor child/ren is awarded to both parties with:

____ **BOTH PARTIES TO SHARE:** Physical care, custody, and control of minor child/ren reasonably between them in a way that ensures minor child/ren are maintaining frequent and continuing contact with both parents.

____ **PRIMARY RESPONSIBILITY:** For care, custody and control of the minor child/ren are to be with: _____ however, _____ shall also have the physical care, custody and control of the minor child/ren during REASONABLE times and for reasonable periods so that the minor child/ren are assured of maintaining frequent and continuing contact with both parents.

____ **PRIMARY RESPONSIBILITY:** For care, custody and control of the minor child/ren are to be with: _____ however, _____ shall have the physical care, custody and control of minor child/ren during the SPECIFIC periods set forth below.

____ **SOLE LEGAL CUSTODY** of minor child/ren shall be awarded to:

_____

____ **REASONABLE:** Visitation with the children is ordered for_____ as set forth below.

____ **SPECIFIC:** Visitation with the children is ordered for _____ as set forth below.

**PHYSICAL CUSTODY:**

____ _____ Shall have sole, physical custody care and control of the minor child/ren.

____ _____ Shall have primary physical custody of the minor child/ren.

____ _____ Shall have secondary physical custody of the minor child/ren.

____ _____ Both parties shall share in the physical care, custody, and control of the minor child/ren reasonably between them in such a manner as to ensure that the minor child/ren maintain frequent and continuing contact with both parents.

____ **Other**:

_____
_____.

## THE MINOR CHILD/REN SHALL BE WITH:

_____

at following time periods:

### REGULAR PERIODS:

___    1.    On alternate weekends:
From:
_____a.m/p.m.
on _____
Until:
_____ a.m/p.m.
on _____
Commencing:
on _____
On three day weekends, the third
day shall be included.


___    2.    On first, second, third, fourth and fifth
weekends of each month:
From:
_____a.m./p.m.
on _____
Until:
_____ a.m./p.m.
on _____
Commencing:
_____

## UNCONVENTIONAL TIME PERIODS:

_____  1.  **Visitation shall be as follows:**
From:
_____a.m./p.m.
on _____
Until:
_____ a.m./p.m.
on _____
Commencing:
on _____

_____  2.  **Other Issues**

_____

_____

_____

_____

_____

_____

_____

_____.

## SCHOOL VACATIONS:

### Child/ren In Year Round Schools:

___ 1. During child/rens' summer, fall, winter and spring school session breaks for a period of ____weeks out of each such break (non-consecutive):
From: _____
Until: _____
With specific dates and times mutually arranged between the parties.

### Child/ren On (9) Month Schedule:

___ 2. For ____ weeks (non consecutive) during summer school vacation of each year:
_____ shall have the right to select dates of the custodial periods in the odd numbered years, and _____ shall have the right to select dates of the summer custodial period in even numbered years.

___ 3. Spring school vacation of each (odd-numbered or even-numbered year:
From: _____ a.m./p.m. on the last day of school prior to vacation:
Until: _____ a.m./p.m. the day before school resumes.

___ 4. **WHEN CHILD/REN ARE WITH:**

_____

during the summer vacation period, then

_____

shall have child/ren:
From:
_____am./p.m.
on _____
Until:
_____am./p.m.
on _____
Commencing:

_____


___ 5. **DURING  SPRING VACATION OF EACH (ODD/EVEN) NUMBERED YEAR:**

_____shall have child/ren:
From:
_____ a.m./p.m.
on the last day of school prior to vacation,

Until:
_____ a.m./p.m.
on the day before school resumes.

## HOLIDAYS:

### Christmas:

_____ 1.     First half of Christmas school vacation:
From:

_____a.m./p.m.
on last day of school before vacation
Until:

_____a.m./p.m.
Christmas Day/Eve in all the even/odd
numbered years.

_____ 2.     Second half of Christmas school vacation:
From:

_____a.m./p.m.
on Christmas Day/Eve
Until:

_____a.m./p.m.
day before school resumes in all
odd/even numbered years.

_____ 3.     On Christmas Day/Eve
From:

_____a.m./p.m.
Until:

_____a.m./p.m.
on Christmas Day/Eve, in
(odd/even) numbered years.
Commencing:

_____

____    4.    **Unconventional Time Periods:**
From:

_____a.m./p.m.
on Christmas Day/Eve.
Until:

_____a.m./p.m.
on Christmas Day/Eve, in
(odd/even) numbered years.
Commencing:

_____

## Thanksgiving:

____    Thanksgiving in all (odd/even) numbered years:
From:

_____a.m./p/m.
on _____
Until:

_____a.m./p.m.
on _____

## Easter:

____    Easter in all (odd/even) numbered years:
From:

_____a.m./p.m.
on _____
Until:

_____a.m./p.m.
on _____
Commencing:

_____

**July 4th:**

\_\_\_\_

On July 4th in all (odd/even) numbered years:
From:

_____a.m./p.m.

on _____

Until:

_____a.m./p.m.

on _____

Commencing _____

## SPECIAL DAYS:
### Birthdays:

\_\_\_\_ 1.

On child/ren's birthday in all (odd/even) numbered years:
From:

_____a.m./p.m.

Until:

_____a.m./p.m.

provided that such time periods do not interfere with the school hours.

\_\_\_\_ 2.

Child/ren shall spend time with mother/father on their birthday each year:
From:

_____ a.m./p.m.

Until:

_____ a.m./p/m.

provided that such time periods do not interfere with the school hours.

## Father's Day/Mother's Day:

____

On Father's Day or Mother's Day (weekend)
of each year child/ren will spend time with
parent on their special day:
From:
_____a.m./p.m.
 on_____
Until:
_____a.m./p.m.
on _____

## Other:

From:
_____a.m./p.m.
on _____
Until:
_____a.m./p.m.
on _____

____

## Explanations:

_____
_____
_____
_____.

## RESTRAINING ORDERS - MINOR CHILD/REN:

_____ 1.  Neither party shall remove minor child/ren from _____ (County/State) without prior written consent of the other party. Or, without prior Court Orders first having been obtained, with the exception of vacation period.

_____ 2.  Neither party shall use, make, or allow any other persons to use, or make disparaging or derogatory remarks about the absent parent in the presence of the child/ren.

_____ 3.  Each party shall keep the other party informed of his/her current address and telephone number and those of the child/ren and shall notify the other parent within a ____ hour period of any change of address or telephone number.

_____ 4.  _____ shall not consume any alcoholic beverage, narcotic, or restricted dangerous drug (except upon prescription) within a ____ hour period prior to or during visitation with the minor child/ren.

## SUPERVISED VISITATION:

____    1.    Supervised visitation with _____ and the minor child/ren shall take place in the presence of:_____.

____    2.    Minor child/ren shall be with _____ at the following times, and at all other times not specifically reserved for _____ above.

## GENERAL VISITATION RULES:

____    1.    Special day contacts shall take precedence over regular periods and holiday visitation for either parent. Holiday contacts shall take precedence over any regular contacts and any school vacation contacts.

____    2.    During any visitation, the non-custodial parent will be expected to spend as much time as possible with the child/ren.

____    3.    Each parent shall carefully avoid the scheduling or arranging of activities for child/ren which are likely to conflict with that visitation or time period that is allocated to the other parent.

____ 4.    The non-custodial parent will give custodial parent twenty-four (24) hours notice in the event he/she is unable to exercise visitation.

____ 5.    The custodial parent will give the non-custodial parent as much notice as is practicable in the event that child/ren are unable to participate in the visitation because of illness.

____ 6.    If the non-custodial parent fails to arrive at the appointed time, then the custodial parent needs to wait only _____ before considering the visitation to have been cancelled.

____ 7.    Child/ren are to be picked up by:

_____

at:_____ a.m./p.m.

and returned by _____

to:_____

at:_____a.m./p.m.

## MEDICAL AND DENTAL:

____ 1. _____is ordered to maintain for the benefit of:

_____ and minor child/ren all medical, dental and hospital insurance (available through employment and/or union affiliation), to reimbursement of any claims under such policy.

____ 2. _____ is ordered to maintain for the benefit of the minor child/ren, named here as follows:

1._____        2._____

3._____        4._____

Medical, dental and hospital insurance (available through either employment and/or through union affiliation) to reimbursement of any claims under such policy.


## EMERGENCY SITUATIONS:

____ Limited to emergency situations, each parent shall be authorized to take any and all actions necessary to protect the health and welfare of their own child/ren, including but not limited to the consent to any emergency surgical procedures or treatment. The parent authorizing such emergency treatment shall notify the other parent within the time period of _____ hours of such an emergency situation and inform the other parent of all the procedures of treatment that were administered to the child/ren.

## BASIC CONDUCT:

1.  Each parent shall keep the other parent advised of his/her current residence address, phone numbers both (home/work), the child/ren's school, location of places where the child/ren will be spending any extended time periods (four days or more). Neither parent shall use such information for harassing or annoying the other parent in any way. Each parent shall be specifically restained and enjoined from disturbing the other's peace or invading the other's privacy by any means whatsoever.

2.  Each party shall be enjoined and restrained from saying or doing anything, or allowing any third person to say or do anything that might tend to alleniate affection of the minor child/ren for the other parent.

3.  Each party shall be enjoined and restrained from making any disparaging remarks about the absent parent in the presence of the minor child/ren.

4.  Each parent is restrained from either harassing, molesting, annoying, striking/hitting, threatening, battering, or disturbing the peace of the other in any manner whatsoever.

5.  Each parent is enjoined and restrained from removing the minor child/ren from original place of residence for the sole purpose of changing child/ren's residence, without prior written consent of the other party, or prior order of the court.

6.  _____shall not consume any alcoholic beverage, narcotics, or restricted drugs (except upon prescription) within _____ hours prior to or during periods of time with the minor child/ren, or allow any third person to do so in the presence of the minor child/ren.

7.  Each party shall be enjoined and restrained from doing anything, or permitting any third party from doing anything, that would be detrimental to the health, safety, morals, or welfare of the minor child/ren.

8.  _____ is/are enjoined and/or restrained from inflicting any corporal punishment or physical discipline of any kind on minor child/ren, or permitting any third person to do so.

9.  _____shall have open telephonic access to the minor child/ren at reasonable times and for reasonable durations, without any third party interference and/or eavesdropping.

10. Each party shall have as much additional time with the minor child/ren as can be agreed upon by the parties.

11. Each party shall notify the other of the name and address of each health practitioner who examines or treat the minor child/ren. Such notification shall be made within _____ days of commencement of the first such treatment or examination.

12. Each party shall have access to the child/ren's school, medical and dental records.

13. In case of an emergency at school:

   _____is the designated person that should be contacted.

**OTHER:**

____ 1. **Parenting Class:**

_____shall enter and
complete an approved parenting class within a
specific period of time, _____
and provide proof of completion by:
_____.


____ 2. **Counseling:**

The minor child/ren:

_____
_____ shall be entered
into                    counseling                    with:
_____ and both parties
shall participate and cooperate at the discretion of
the therapist. A report from the therapist shall be
available to the court at the next court date.

____ 3. **Psychological Evaluation:**

The parties shall participate in a psychological
evaluation to be performed by:
_____.
Each party stipulates that the evaluation report
may be admitted into evidence at further hearing
or trial without foundation and over any hearsay
objection, and subject to each party's right of cross
examination.

## MODIFICATIONS/SUPPLEMENTS TO SPECIFIC ORDERS:

\_\_\_\_ 1. The order modifies and supersedes all previous orders concerning custody of and contacts with the minor child/ren.

\_\_\_\_ 2. This is a supplement to previous orders made. Previous orders that concern custody, visitation, or contact with the minor child/ren that are not inconsistent with these orders shall remain in full force and effect.

\_\_\_\_ **OTHER ORDERS:**

_____

_____

_____

_____.

## RESIDENCY RESTRICTION

\_\_\_\_ The child/ren's residence will be restricted to the county of _____unless there is a written agreement of the parties or an order of the court.

**Note:** This residency restriction clause precludes the custodial parent from moving in an attempt to thwart contact with the child/ren.

## CHAPTER 16

# REFORMS NEEDED

"Until death do us part" does not really mean what it says. Today, marriages only last until someone better comes along or until the money runs out. All it takes is one person wanting out of the marriage for the family unit blow apart and children become victims. "I never loved you" becomes the battle cry and is heard by most fathers and most children. No fault, easy divorce, has changed childhood from a warm, happy, snuggly, time of life, to life in a free fire combat zone. Children suffer the most, yet they have no say when their parents separate.

Children should be guaranteed an opportunity to voice their wishes when parents separate. The single most important event of a child's life is made without any input from the child. A child is allowed to give suggestions as to: Schools, extracurricular activities, friends, social events, and all of the other elements that affect the way they grow up.

# EASY DIVORCE

Easy divorce is a recent phenomena in the history of the world, and many countries do not allow divorce. Our government gives parents the freedom to walk away from a marriage, despite the damage which might affect the children. This system causes children to suffer, progresses to dysfunctional children growing up to be dysfunctional adults, and yet children have no say. This cycle of pain results in billions of dollars spent for government programs to offset the damage of the breakup of the family unit. The divorce process benefits attorneys, psychiatrists, accountants, dating services, and singles bars, but destroys children.

The ultimate solution for the crime, welfare, and poverty in this country is to preserve the family unit. The legislative branch of government must keep in step with the radical changes that have taken place in today's society. Our government should spend more money on the prevention of broken homes, rather than on the effects of broken homes.

New laws need to be enacted that would put fathers on an equal footing with mothers when embroiled in a custody battle. The goal of 50/50 shared parenting should become the law across this nation. Family law judges would then have the duty of dividing up the time periods.

**Note:** Laws have always followed slowly behind societal changes. Today's custody laws are not keeping up with a society that is evolving:

"Faster Than A Speeding Bullet"

1.     **COUNSELING COURSE BEFORE DIVORCE:**

Mandated divorce counseling should be required before a parent can request a divorce when there are children. All counseling would focus on the needs of the children and methods to lessen the animosity between parents. Parents would have to prove that the divorce would not harm the children in order to graduate.

No Diploma - No Divorce

2.     **NO DIVORCE UNTIL CHILDREN IN SCHOOL:**

Neither parent should be allowed to file for a divorce until the youngest child is in school full time. Studies show that preschoolers depend on both parents in their primary years for nurturing, sustenance, and personality development. Children at this early age have little contact with anyone other than their parents, and relatives during preschool years. The parent's desires will just have to wait.

This reform would result in a burden to parents wanting out of a marriage, but the benefits to children and society will greatly outweigh the inconvenience. Parents electing to have a child, would know the birth of a child requires a five-year commitment to the relationship. This would guarantee children two full-time parents until school age.

3.     **CHILDREN OUT OF WEDLOCK:**

Fathers who procreate children, without marrying the mother, should be required to become actively involved in the child's life. The government should get out of the business of paying for the raising of children. Fatherhood is an innate longing that should be allowed to flourish. A father that truly wants nothing to do with his children should be given the choice of a chain gang or Devil's Island.

Forced parenting should be applicable to all parents, fathers and mothers alike. Fathers refusing to spend time nurturing their children should have to pick up trash on the freeways for double the parenting time avoided.

4.     **PARENTING LICENSE:**

Parenting skills should be given more attention than driving skills. It takes classes, practice, and a test to get a drivers license, yet parents walk out of a hospital, with an infant child, no instruction booklet, no experience, and no supervision. No governmental agency oversees the welfare of children.

We are at a point in history where a mother giving birth does not have accountability for the child. Historically, the family, village, and tribe would all assist in raising children. Today, a mother can leave the hospital, stop by the welfare office, and is accountable to no one.

5.    CHILD SUPPORT TO CHILDREN:

Child support monies should go toward the benefit of the children. A national trust fund should be set up, and child support would go directly from wages into the child's trust account. The custodial parent should be accountable for all funds and these funds must be used for the children. The non-custodial parent should receive an accounting from the custodial parent, and have the opportunity to audit how the funds are used. Misuse of funds should result in an automatic switch of custody.

It is a financial windfall to have custody of the children when child support is more than the amount actually spent on the children. This financial gain is often the real reason for many custody battles. Mom wants custody of the children because of the money that comes with them.


6.    CUSTODY TO DAD IF MOM ON WELFARE:

If mom is unable to raise the children without government funds, dad should be given custody. Switching custody to dad would be automatic when mom applies for welfare. Taxpayers would save billions of dollars each year and moms would have incentive to earn a living, which in turn, would break the welfare cycle.

Dads should be identified at the time of the child's birth, named on the birth certificate, logged into a computer, and the welfare department would contact dad immediately when mom applied for welfare.

7.   **ALL PARENTS MUST PAY:**

Moms rarely pay child support when a dad gets custody of the children. Statistics are kept regarding child support to moms, but not to dads. Wisconsin is the only state that keeps statistics on child support to dads. The statistics show that a meager 30% of dads with custody are awarded child support as compared with 80% of custodial moms being awarded child support. Automatic payments should be deducted through wage garnishment regardless of gender.

8.   **SCHOOL RECORDS TO BOTH PARENTS:**

All school records should automatically be sent to both parents. Each parent should have equal right to children's involvement at school and/or daycare. Both parents should be guaranteed the right to school records and be informed of the children's academic progress, behavior, and school activities.

Both parents should receive all school notices regarding: Teacher conferences, progress reports, report cards, class photographs, newsletters about upcoming school events such as: School plays, concerts, sporting events, and fund raising activities. Both parents names should be listed on school emergency card so that when an emergency arises. Each parent should be notified in case of an accident, health, or illness problem with their children.

## 9.    ADULTERY PENALIZED

You can sue someone that crashes into your yard, but you cannot sue someone screwing your wife. Children should be allowed to sue an adult who blows up the family unit. There is no penalty for adultery. Adults have the freedom to have sex with anyone they want. Adultery results in broken relationships which results in broken homes which results in broken children. Because of this, children suffer from intentional misconduct with no compensation for the emotional damage inflicted upon them.

The offending sex partner has nothing to lose. A family is destroyed and you can't even sue the bastard. You should be able to make him pay for the intentional suffering to the mental damage to the children. Opening the doors of litigation would stop the adultery.

## 10.    LIFESTYLE RESTRICTIONS:

A parent's lifestyle should be restricted when it adversely affects the children. Second hand smoke causes over 200,000 cases a year of bronchitis in children under 18 months of age, and over 10,000 of these cases result in hospitalization. Children should not be subjected to any health risk caused by smoking adults. Adult conduct that is detrimental to the health of children, should result in a criminal offense and they should be fully prosecuted.

## 11. CHILD RIGHTS LEGISLATION:

Child rights legislation should be enacted to ensure that the basic rights of children are protected. Children should have a Bill of Rights. Government spends massive amounts on the affects of family breakdowns rather than preventive measures: Job training, drug rehabilitation, institutions and jails. The cost in dollars and the childhood suffering should trigger governmental intervention. Irreversible damage can be avoided.

Laws regarding children should be administered by an independent governmental agency that gets opinions from children. Children old enough to talk should be given a meaningful voice in custody decisions. This legislation would help children cope and guarantee them the right to grow up in the household of their choice. Children have suffered long enough and it is time for change.

## 12. FEDERAL CUSTODY LAWS:

Children are entitled to uniform custody laws, no matter the state in which they reside. Custody laws are presently decided by each individual state which, in turn,results in a checkerboard pattern of custody laws throughout this nation.

State laws should be abolished in the area of custody and a uniform federal law should be enacted. All children would be treated equally and our mobile society would not be faced with different laws in different states. Federal law would ensure standardized guidelines that would be consistent throughout the country.

The legal system's attempt to preserve the rights of parents often has devastating effects on the lives of children. Legislators should begin right now in drafting laws that protect the rights of children first, and secondarily the parents. New laws are needed to break this continuous cycle of dysfunctional children caused by divorces, so that children do not repeat the errors of their parents.

Our nation's children deserve to grow up in a wholesome environment, and not be used as pawns in a custody battle fueled by greed and revenge. Children are entitled to live with the better parent, rather than being forced to live with the one selected by a legal system that has little or no knowledge of the case. A system that routinely grants custody to the mother.

Fathers have the right to receive equal consideration in the lives of their children. Not only will children benefit, but so too, will the social fabric of this nation strengthen.

## CHAPTER 17

# FATHERS RESOURCES

Fathers are now forming groups, banding together, and sharing information in the quest for equal rights as a parent. This positive interaction is giving fathers a place to turn for help when involved in custody litigation. This recent boom in the fatherhood movement is because of the groundswell of fathers fighting back.

With every family breakup, there is a residency change. The big question is, how far the move-away. This potential for being disconnected from the children will dramatically increase the number of fathers seeking custody. The days of an automatic win for mothers are over. Fathers who are prepared and persistent will prevail, and eventually the family law courts will become an even playing field.

Help is available for embattled fathers. The fathers rights movement is growing rapidly and only needs a charismatic speaker to be on equal footing with the impressive feminist movement. In less than one generation, women are close to equality in the workforce and this accomplishment can be duplicated in the father's rights movement. Exchange of information, leading to changes in the law, resulting in a new way of thinking is how the father's rights movement will prevail.

There is a tremendous need for a national clearing center and an umbrella group to coordinate the underfunded efforts of individual fathers and groups. More and more books and materials on male issues are being written than ever before. All bookstores and libraries are shelved with hundreds of titles for women, but not for men. Ask your community bookstore and library to set up a men's section. The pressure on libraries and bookstores to stock male oriented materials, will cause authors to write more books aimed at a male audience, particularly custody issues. The result will be a larger body of knowledge for fathers seeking assistance in custody litigation.

Listed are newspapers, magazines, newsletters, books, and organizations on male related topics. This list is intended to help you with your individual situation, and offer you a place to go for additional information.

**Note:** We will gladly provide you with the names and telephone numbers of fathers' rights groups in your area. Please let us know of any new groups, legislation, case law, activities, etc., for distribution.

## NEWSPAPERS AND MAGAZINES

*Children's Advocate* - A 20-page monthly newsletter published by the New Jersey Council For Children's Rights, Box 316 Pluckemin, New Jersey 07978-0316, (973) 694-9323. Affiliated with Children's Rights Council (CRC). Lists meetings and events in New Jersey area. Feature articles Include: Hands On Fathers; Things You Have Wanted To Tell A Judge But Didn't Dare; Child Kidnapping; Walk Away Wives and many other topical articles. Invaluable statistical information. $1.95 per issue.

*Family Bulletin* - A 15-page newspaper published monthly by Coalition of Parent Support (C.O.P.S.) 2214 Arden Way, Suite 197, Sacramento, California 95825. (805) 588-2677. E-mail: cops@eee.org. WEBSITE: www.copps.org. *Family Bulletin* has the most up-to-date information on new legislative changes and bills related to family law issues. Membership $50.00 per year.

*Fathers & Families* - A 12-page newspaper published quarterly by *Fathers & Families*, P.O. Box 67398, Los Angeles, California, 90067. Editor, Dianna Thompson, (800)-752-6562 Ext. 221. E-mail 73674.1710@compuserve.com. Feature articles: Fatherhood Is On The Rise, No Democracy Without Dads, Women In The Fathers Movement. Invaluable statistics, research, and studies information. Book reviews and Letters to the Editors. Affiliated with the American Coalition For Fathers And Children (ACFC).

*Fathers National Review* - A 25-page newspaper published periodically by Dads Against Discrimination, The Oregon Pioneer Bldg., 320 SW Stark Street, Suite 516, Portland, Oregon 92704-2632, (503) 222-1111. E-mail: dads@teleport.com. WEBSITE: www.teleport.com/~dads/. Feature articles Include: Fathers Must Demand Sole Custody Not Joint Custody, Divorce Related Malicious Mother Syndrome, The Child Support Enforcement Program. State by state summary of Father's Rights activities and interests. Subscription $5.00 per issue.

*__Full-Time Dads__* - A 25-page magazine published bimonthly. *Full-Time Dads,* 193 Shelley Avenue, Elizabeth, New Jersey 07208. James McLoughlin, Publisher/Editor (908)-355-9722, E-mail: FTDMAG@aol.com WEBSITE: www.parentcity.com. Single issue is $5.00 or subscription is $20.00 per year.

*__Liberator__* - A 25-page newspaper published monthly by the Men's Defense Association, 17854 Lyons St. Forest Lake, MN. 55025-8107. (612)-464-7887. E-mail: rdoyle@mensdefense.org. or info@mensdefense.org. WEBSITE: www.mensdefense.com. The nations foremost men's movement news forum. Feature articles include: Welfare Fraud And Failure; Taxes And Divorce; Life Without Father; and reviews recent court cases. Letters to the Editor, and gives a synopsis of nationally published father articles. Mail order literature on fathers' rights available. Subscription $24.00 per year.

*__Men's Stuff__* - A 25-page newsletter published quarterly by The National Men's Resource Center, Box 800-HL, San Anselmo, California 94979-0800, Gordon Clay, President. (415) 453-2839. WEBSITE: www.menstuff.org. The most complete listing of men's events around the country and brings 100 men's issues into public awareness through media, workshops and conferences. Lists hundreds of services and organizations for men nationwide. Sponsors The Browser Book Mobile that holds 1,200 books on men related issues. The Book Mobile travels around the country visiting libraries, bookstores, and colleges in rural communities. Subscription, $10.00 per year.

*__Speaking Out For Children__* - A 20-page newsletter published quarterly by The Children's Rights Council, Inc., 6200 Editors Park Drive, Suite 103, Hyattsville, MD 20782, David Levy, Esq., President (301) 559-3120 Fax (301) 559-3124. Articles include: Governmental Bills And Resolutions In Congress, summarizes nationwide cases, and reports on statewide children's issues. Lists national affiliate organizations and chapters in 31 states. Subscription included with CRC membership.

***Team Works*** - A monthly newsletter listing the bi-monthly FREE workshops provided by Teamworks in San Diego. 1450 Frazee Road, Suite 307, San Diego, California.92108. (800) 781-1980. E-mail: info@teamworks.com. Newsletter has a humorous poem or story related to the theme of the speaker for the "3rd Saturday" workshop. Newsletter also includes: Monthly schedule of classes, mediation information, parenting tips, and fees for filing services.

***Today's Dad*** - An 8-page monthly newsletter published by Wisconsin Fathers For Equal Justice, (WFEJ) P.O. Box 1742, Madison, Wisconsin 53701. (608) ALL-DADS. E-mail: buyright@execpc.com.WEBSITE: www.execp.com/wismen/wfej Accepts unsolicited articles and letters to the editor for print. Articles include helping fathers normalize family relationships with children when parents are no longer living together. Free subscription to all family law courts, counseling services, commissioners, judges, legislators, and prison libraries of Wisconsin and members of WFEJ. Non-members $30.00 yearly.

***Today's Father*** - A 15-page magazine published by National Center for Fathering, 10200 West 75th Street, Suite 267, Shawnee Mission, Kansas 66204, Dr. Ken Canfield, President (913) 384-4661, E-mail: www.fathers.com. WEBSITE: www.fathers.com. Feature articles include: Nurturing BecomesThe Man; Father Figures Change As Men Grow; The Perks Of Spiritual Oneness. Mail order books, articles and tapes. Subscription by donation.

***Transitions*** - Journal of men's perspective published bimonthly by the National Coalition of Free Men, P.O. Box 129 Manhasset, New York 11030. Tom Williamson, President. (516) 482-6378. E-mail: ncfm@ncfm.org. WEBSITE: www.ncfm.org. Notices regarding national fathers' rights events, letters to the editor, and highly opinionated editorials. Listing of state representatives with phone numbers. Membership to NCFM organization is $30.00 per year includes subscription or $2.00 per issue.

# BOOKS

## Divorce Sourcebook

***DIVORCE HELP SOURCEBOOK*** Author: Engel, Marjorie Available in major book stores and Visible Ink Press, 835 Penobscot Building, Detroit MI. 48226-4095, (800)-877-4253. The undisputed leading authority and the most comprehensive resource guide available for individuals seeking information on divorce. Each section offers an exhaustive collection of books, publications and lists of divorcing resources. The yellow pages of divorce, if it's out there, it's here. Price: $17.95.

## False Molestation

***DON'T BLAME ME, DADDY,*** False Accusations Of Child Sexual Abuse   Author: Tong, Dean Available in major book stores and through Children of Divorce and Separation (CODAS, Inc.) (215)-576-0177 or Fax (215)-576-9411. Email: DrKenLewis @juno.com. Dean Tong is a nationally recognized leader in the area of child advocacy and an expert on this subject. Insight into the courts and child protection systems. A must read for anyone accused of false allegations of sex abuse. This book should be required reading for all social workers, psychologists, attorneys, judges, and police officers. Price: $11.95.

## Father Power

***THE GARBAGE GENERATION*** Author: Amneus, Daniel Primrose Press, 2131 So. Primrose Ave., Alhambra, CA. 91803. An outstanding study on consequences of the destruction of the two parent family and need to stabilize it by strengthening its weakest link, father's role. Term, garbage generation, refers to children growing up in female headed households. Price $12.00.

## Fatherlessness

*FATHERLESS AMERICA*, Confronting Our Most Urgent Social Problem, Author: Blankenhorn, David.
Available in all bookstores, and from Basic Books, 10 East 53rd St., New York, New York, 10022-5299.
Mr. Blankenhorn confronts our most urgent social problem, fatherlessness, and gives a history of evolution of fatherhood and diminishment in our American society. This book is an encyclopedia of references and statistics on fatherlessness in our nation. Chapters include: The Deadbeat Dad; The Visiting Father; The Sperm Father; The Unnecessary Father; The Stepfather And Near-by Guy. Price $23.00.

## Parenting During Divorce

*PUTTING KIDS FIRST*, Walking Away From A Marriage Without Walking Over The Kids Author: Oddenino, Michael Family Connections Publishing 575 East 4500 So. Suite B-250 Saltlake City, Utah, or Oddenino & Gaule 444 East Huntington Drive, Suite 325, Arcadia, CA. 91006.
This excellent guidebook helps parents keep their own children out of the explosions of the divorcing process. Offers a child's Bill of Rights, sample Custody Agreement, and gives ten suggestions in post-divorce parenting. Price: $16.95.

## Paternity

*MAMA'S BABY...DADDY'S MAYBE?* A Handbook For The Alleged Father Author: Snipes, J. Toy
Available from Think Big Productions, Box 2978 Inglewood, CA. 90305, (213) 752-7595.
A handbook for those 300,000 males annually who are slapped with paternity suits. Children For Profit, Blood Testing, Child Support, Laws Concerning Paternity and Child Support. Price $5.95.

## Recovery From Divorce

*HEALING HEARTS,* Helping Children And Adults Recover From Divorce Author: Hickey, Elizabeth and Dalton, Elizabeth Gold Leaf Press, 2533 No. Carson St. Ste. 1544 Carson City, NV. 89706, (1-800) 748-4900.
A manual that is widely used in courses created for divorcing parents. Advice for helping children through the divorce process in the most humane manner possible. Practical information for counselors and parents. Price $19.95.

## Teenage Fatherhood

*TEEN DADS,* Rights Responsibilities And Joys
Lindsay, Jeanne W., Morning Glory Press, 6595 San Haroldo Way, Buena Park, CA. 90620-3748 (714) 828-1998
A handbook that communicates at the maturity level of teenage fathers. It is designed to teach young fathers responsible and joyful parenting. Chapters include: Baby's Development Before Birth; Caring For Your Newborn; Good Food For Babies And Toddlers. Price $9.95.

# NATIONAL ORGANIZATIONS

## AMERICAN COALITION FOR FATHERS AND CHILDREN

**(ACFC)** 22365 El Toro Road, Suite 335, Lake Forest, California 92630, Dianna Thompson, Vice President, (800) 978 DADS. For California Chapter (949) 859-7000 Fax (949)-455-2677.E-mail: ACFCmember@aol.com. WEBSITE: www.acfc.org.

A nationwide, nonprofit organization representing the rights of non-custodial parents, second wives, and grandparents. ACFC is composed of men and women who believe that regardless of martial status, children benefit from the on-going emotional, physical, and financial support of both parents. ACFC has chapters and affiliate organizations in several states. Membership is $75.00. Includes ACFC's membership manual, Shared parenting Tool-Kit written by national leading experts in all areas of interest to the non-custodial parent, numerous resources, website access with research, studies, and statistical information, and *Fathers and Families* newspaper.

## CHILDREN'S RIGHTS COUNCIL 6200 Editors Park Drive,

Suite 103 Hyattsville, MD. 20782, David Levy, Esq., President, (301) 559-3120 Fax (301) 559-3124. WEBSITE: www.gocrc.com and www.info4parents.com E-Mail: crcdc@erols.com.

A nationwide, nonprofit children's rights organization that works to strengthen families through education. CRC promotes family preservation, but if families breakup work to assure a child's right to have continued and meaningful contact with both parents, extended family, and especially grandparents. CRC motto, "The Best Parent Is Both Parents." CRC holds annual conferences with nationally prominent speakers on custody issues, reform, mediation, parenting, and financial child support. CRC has chapters nationwide, and has a directory listing of over 1,200 organizations in the U.S. and abroad involved with problems that affect children of divorce. Catalog of over 100 book resources, written reports, audio cassettes, model bills, and gifts for children. CRC annual membership is $35.00. Includes quarterly newsletter, *Speaking Out For Children.*

**DADS AGAINST DISCRIMINATION** 732 South West 3rd Avenue Suite 405, Portland, Oregon 97204, Joe Martel. (503)-222-1111. E-mail: dads@teleport.com. WEBSITE: www.teleport.com/~dads/. A nonprofit organization created by both divorced and unwedded fathers for the benefit of all fathers. Promoting the belief that fathers need an informational resource center concerning fathers' rights. Offer remedies during the stressful periods of the family breakup. Services include: A telephone crisis line for fathers, call-in cable TV program, distribution of videotapes, has meetings informing fathers of pending governmental regulations, gives information about court documents/forms, has a referral source to attorneys/psychologists, and do extensive research on the positive impact of fathers on family. Publishes *Fathers National Review*

**FATHERLINK** - National Center on Fathers and Families, University of Pennsylvania, 3440 Market Street, Suite 450, Philadelphia, PA. 19104, Vivian L.Gadsden, Executive Director. (215) 573-5500 E-mail: mailbox@ncoff.gse.upenn.edu. WEBSITE: www.ncoff.gse.upen.edu/link. The Fatherlink project is aimed at unifying the field of fathers and families by collaborating and encouraging communication across research, practice, and policy domains. The LINK provides a site where current, accurate information can be located, posted, and discussed by a variety of professionals and other individuals committed to the study, support and strengthening of families. The LINK is maintained by (NCOFF) and is available both within HandsNet's Children, Youth, and Families Forum. WEBSITE: www.handsnet.org. and at a public access Internet site. A resource developed for and by the father and family community. We are always seeking information to add to our site.

**FATHERNET** - Children, Youth, and Family Consortium, 270A McNamara Alumni Center – 200 Oak Street South East, Minneapolis, MN. 55455. Rebecca Reibestein. (612) 625-7849. Fax (612) 625-7815 E-mail: cyfc@tc.umn.edu. WEBSITE: www.cyfc.umn.edu/Fathernet. Fathernet provides information on the importance of fathers and fathering and how fathers can be good parents and parent educators. It includes research, policy and opinion documents to inform users about the factors that support and hinder men's involvement in the lives of children. Fathernet also provides an Electronic Discussion Group to increase the number and diversity of voices discussing fatherhood and the importance of men's involvement in the lives of children, and hopefully to move our nation toward policies and action.

**FATHERS RIGHTS & EQUALITY EXCHANGE (F.R.E.E.) & F.R.E.E. FOUNDATION** 2700 West Evans Avenue, Suite 850 Denver, CO. 80219. Kenneth Ward, (303) 937-3911. E-mail: user742@aol.com
An organization dedicated to the premise that parenting is a 50/50 proposition. Both parents should share equally in the parenting and financial support of their children. *WE MAKE CUSTODIAL FATHERS*. We offer advice and assistance in divorce/custody issues, through local coordinators, and maintain a very active computer network of father connection resources and a lively mailing list. Membership $50.00. *"F.R.E.E. Thoughts"* newsletter available upon request.

**JOINT CUSTODY ASSOCIATION** 10606 Wilkins Avenue, Los Angeles, CA. 90024 James Cook, President (310) 475-5352. A nonprofit organization with twenty years' experience in helping parents, attorneys and therapists to create custody solutions. Initiates legislation to modify divorce laws aimed at custody equality. Assists individuals and fathers' organizations to grow by providing informed contacts, networking and research. Mr. Cook speaks regularly across the country to many organizations and has been effective in providing testimony and advice to legislatures. With 4,000 members in 43 states and 15 foreign countries, the Joint Custody Association compiles kits containing 180 different items totaling 800 pages providing in-depth information on 38 issues of custody and divorce. A $40.00 contribution to JCA includes membership, 800 page kit, and subscription to *Joint Custodian,* a periodic newsletter updating recent developments for recipients of the initial kit.

**MEN'S DEFENSE ASSOCIATION** 17854 Lyons Street, Forest Lake, Minnesota 55025, Richard R. Doyle, President, (651) 464-7887. E-mail: rdoyle@mensdefense.org. or info@mensdefense. WEBSITE: www.mensdefense.org.
A nonprofit group founded in 1972 to help men in divorce and all instances of anti-male prejudice. The nation's foremost men's movement news forum. Provides booklets on various divorce and gender issues. National television and radio personality quoted in prestigious magazines. Clearing house for information on fathers' issues. Mail order items available and include: fathers' rights books, monographs, habeas corpus forms, support guidelines, and bumper stickers. *The Liberator* is an international men's unity newsmagazine. Membership $20.00, and subscription to *The Liberator* is $24.00 per year.

**NATIONAL CENTER FOR FATHERING** 10200 W. 75th St. #267, Shawnee Mission, Kansas. 66204, Dr. Ken Canfield, President. (913) 384-4661. E-mail: www.fathers.com. WEBSITE: www.fathers.com. Dr. Canfield is a research scholar specializing in the area of fatherhood and history of the family. Dr. Canfield serves as president of the Kansas City-based National Center For Fathering, which is a nonprofit education and research center dedicated to inspiring and equipping men to be responsible fathers. Dr. Canfield is also the author of two books; *The Seven Secrets of Effective Fathers*, and *The Heart of a Father*. He is recognized as an authority on fathering skills, research, and the negative consequences of fatherlessness. National Center for Fathering has a quarterly magazine, *Today's Father* and also a weekday radio commentary, *Today's Father*. To be included on mailing list contact our E-mail or Website. A suggested donation of $15.00 will be appreciated.

**NATIONAL FATHERHOOD INITIATIVE** 101 Lake Forest Blvd – Suite 360, Gaithersburg, MD. 20878, (301) 948-0599 or (800) 970 DADS, Fax (301) 984-4325. Dr. Wade F. Horn, Pres. E-mail: info@fatherhood.org. WEBSITE: www.fatherhood.org. The mission of the National Fatherhood Initiative is to improve the well being of children in America by increasing the number of children raised by responsible, committed and loving fathers. The National Fatherhood Resource Center and Clearinghouse offers technical assistance to grass-roots fatherhood organizations and assistance to communities and states seeking to develop new programs or policies for encouraging responsible fatherhood.

## NEW JERSEY COUNCIL FOR CHILDREN'S RIGHTS
(NJCCR) P. O. Box 391 Bloomsburg, New Jersey, 08804 (201) 434-7938. Eric Purasson, Pres. WEBSITE: www.njccr.org. A non-profit corporation established to focus on the rights of children to have meaningful relationships with both parents. Our goals are to develop and make available educational resources for divorced parents on a variety of issues as they relate to their children. Parenting plans, custody options, child support issues, parenting time, and out of state removal are a few of our concerns. We serve as a vehicle to legislators, courts, social services, schools and others who deal with the disruption of the family unit.

**TEAMWORKS** – 1450 Frazee Road, Suite 307, San Diego, California 92108, Deena Stacer, Executive Director. (800) 781-1980, Fax (619) 299-7136.E-mail: info@teamworksdivorce.com. WEBSITE: www.teamworksdivorce.com.
Teamworks gives two free bi-monthly workshops in San Diego County, where family law attorneys answer questions and provide direction to attendees to resolve their case. Teamworks also offers affordable filing for San Diego County family law cases and Mediation Services. We have an Education Resource Center with information and resources to assist with: Family law issues, parenting, positive discipline, single, blended and step family issues. Included in the Education Resource Center are articles on mediation, team building, relationship and communication skills, and "high-conflict divorce." Teamworks has developed a high-conflict program that educates both professionals involved with the court system and the families going through a high conflict divorce or break-up.

**WISCONSIN FATHERS FOR EQUAL JUSTICE** Box 1742, Madison, Wisconsin 53701, Jim Novak, President (608) ALL DADS. WEBSITE: www.execpc.com/wismen/wfej. A nonprofit organization aimed at helping fathers and their children normalize family relationships when parents do not live together. Promotes legislation that seeks to create a rebuttable presumption that both parents are fit and capable of raising their children, as well as a fundamental right of each parent to spend equal time periods with their children. Jim Novak is also the author of *Wisconsin Father's guide to Divorce and Custody* written specifically for Wisconsin. WFEJ publishes a newsletter, *Today's Dads*, which is distributed without charge to all family law courts, counseling services, prison libraries, legislators, commissioners, judges, in the state of Wisconsin and members of WFEJ. Membership $30.00 Available to non-members, $30.00 per year.

# ORDER FORM

Please send _____ copies of *Custody for Fathers* to:

Name:_____

Address:_____

City: _____ State: ____ Zip _____

Telephone (____)_____

**Postal Orders:**

LAW OFFICES OF MICHAEL BRENNAN
250 East 17th Street
Costa Mesa, CA. 92627

**Telephone Orders:** 949-646-9842
**Fax Orders:** 949-646-3453

**Sales Price** $24.95 **Sales Tax:** Add 7.75% shipped to
California addresses
**Shipping:** $3.00

**Payment:**
__ Cheque
__ Credit Card: __ Visa __ MasterCard __Amex

Card Number:

_____

Name On Card: _____
Expiration Date: _____

# ORDER FORM

Please send _____ copies of *Custody for Fathers* to:

Name:_____

Address:_____

City: _____ State: ____ Zip _____

Telephone (____)_____

**Postal Orders:**

LAW OFFICES OF MICHAEL BRENNAN
250 East 17th Street
Costa Mesa, CA. 92627

**Telephone Orders:**   949-646-9842
**Fax Orders:**          949-646-3453

**Sales Price**   $24.95  **Sales Tax:**   Add 7.75% shipped to
                                           California addresses
**Shipping:**     $3.00

**Payment:**
__ Cheque
__ Credit Card: __ Visa __ MasterCard __ Amex

Card Number:

_____

Name On Card: _____

Expiration Date: _____